YOU DESERVE DESSERT!

Member Recipes

Cooking Club
of
America

Wacky Cake with Caramel Icing (page 13)

You Deserve Dessert!

Printed in 2011.

Tom Carpenter
Creative Director

Lisa Golden Schroeder
Recipe Editor and Food Stylist

Jennifer Weaverling
Managing Editor

Mowers Photography
Commissioned Photography

Wendy Holdman
Cover Design

Peter Bischoff
Photo Assistant

Laura Holle
Book Development Assistant

Kimberly Colburn
Pegi Lee
Assistant Food Stylists

Zachary Marell
Book Design and Production

On Cover: Lemon-Cream Cheese Pound Cake, page 112
On Back Cover: Raspberry Pie, page 32
    Sour Cream Cut-Out Cookies, page 65
    Espresso Bread Pudding with Almond-Flavored Liqueur Custard Sauce, page 99
On Page 1: Wine Braised Pear Chantilly, page 133

4 5 6 / 15 14 13 12 11
© 2010 Cooking Club of America
ISBN 13: 978-1-58159-501-7

Cooking Club of America
12301 Whitewater Drive
Minnetonka, MN 55343
www.cookingclub.com

Double Chocolate Fudge Cake (page 109)

Mini Cheesecakes (page 128)

CONTENTS

INTRODUCTION

Frozen Pudding Sandwiches (page 144)

Go Ahead ... You Deserve DESSERT!

Since we were little, we've heard all about the foods that are good for us: milk for strong bones and teeth, carrots for sharp eyes, protein-rich meat to build muscles, pasta and breads for energy. Most of us can recite many more items from that long list.

But there's one glaring absence from the litany of "good for you" things, one important food item that never really qualified for the list: dessert. No kidding!

How can *dessert* be good for someone? What does dessert take care of in the scheme of things? Simple. Dessert just makes you feel good ... an important food for the soul, a little break from reality and rules.

Yes, there's usually sugar involved, which of course means some calories. But if it tastes great, you love eating it and it makes you feel good, what's wrong with something sweet—a little dessert—now and again? You deserve it.

Those were our simple sentiments as we at the Cooking Club of America created this book. And when it came time to name the pages you're holding, we thought why not call it like we see it: *You Deserve DESSERT!*

Grandma Betty's Upside-Down Cobbler (page 37)

Crème De Menthe Brownies with a Crust (page 85)

You can thank your fellow members for this book. They're the ones that provided recipes by the hundreds. In fact, the hardest part about our job was whittling down all those submissions into the 253-recipe package you're holding. Not an easy task!

You'll find it all here—awesome items for dessert, and goodies and sweets beyond the dinner table. Great cakes for occasions casual and fancy. Pies and cobblers. Cookies, bars and brownies. Puddings and custards and other creamy creations. Cheesecakes and many other special desserts. Ice creams, and sauces to go with them. Plus candies, confections and other sweet treats.

This may not be a cookbook you pull out and use every day, and that's fine. But it *is* a resource of ideas that will keep you creating wonderful desserts—and feeling good about them—for a long time to come.

You work hard, and love to cook. Don't shy away from one of the foods you love that also makes you happy. You deserve DESSERT!

GREAT CAKES &

SWEET BREADS

BLUEBERRY TEA CAKE
WITH LEMON SAUCE (page 16)

VOLCANO CAKE

RANDEE ECKSTEIN
LITTLE NECK, NEW YORK

CAKE

2½ cups all-purpose flour

1½ cups sugar

½ cup unsweetened cocoa

2 teaspoons baking soda

½ teaspoon salt

⅔ cup vegetable oil

2 tablespoons apple cider vinegar

1 tablespoon vanilla

2 cups cold coffee

TOPPING

⅓ cup sugar

1 teaspoon cinnamon

1 Heat oven to 350°F. Stir together flour, 1½ cups sugar, cocoa, baking soda and salt. Make 3 depressions in dry mixture. Pour oil into one depression, cider vinegar into another, and vanilla into third depression. Pour coffee over entire surface; mix well.

2 Spread evenly in 13x9-inch pan. In small bowl, stir ⅓ cup sugar and cinnamon together; sprinkle one-half of topping over cake.

3 Bake 30 to 40 minutes or until toothpick inserted in center comes out clean. Sprinkle with remaining topping. Cool 20 minutes before serving.

16 servings

GINGERBREAD WITH HOT FUDGE SAUCE

KAY SPARKMAN
ALEXANDRIA, VIRGINIA

BREAD

½ cup butter, softened

½ cup sugar

2 eggs

1 cup molasses

2 cups all-purpose flour

1 teaspoon ground ginger

1 teaspoon cinnamon

1 teaspoon ground cloves

1 teaspoon salt

1 teaspoon baking soda

1 cup hot water

SAUCE

2 (1-oz.) squares unsweetened chocolate

1 tablespoon butter

⅓ cup boiling water

2 tablespoons light corn syrup

⅓ cup sugar

1 teaspoon vanilla

1 Heat oven to 350°F. Spray 9-inch round cake pan with nonstick cooking spray.

2 In large bowl, beat ½ cup butter and ½ cup sugar at medium-high speed until fluffy. Add eggs; beat well. Add molasses; beat well.

3 In another large bowl, mix flour, ginger, cinnamon, cloves and salt. Dissolve baking soda in 1 cup hot water. Gradually add and stir in flour mixture alternately with water and soda, starting and ending with dry ingredients. Pour into pan.

4 Bake 30 minutes or until toothpick inserted in center comes out clean. Cool in pan on wire rack.

5 To prepare sauce, melt chocolate and 1 tablespoon butter with ⅓ cup water in medium saucepan over medium heat; stir until smooth. Add syrup and ⅓ cup sugar. Increase heat to medium-high, stirring occasionally until boiling. Reduce heat to medium-low. Allow mixture to simmer exactly 8 minutes without stirring. Dip saucepan briefly in cold water. Stir in vanilla. Serve warm over gingerbread with vanilla ice cream, if desired. Store in refrigerator.

8 servings

MISSISSIPPI MUD CAKE

LENA RICE
BOISE, IDAHO

CAKE

2 cups sugar

1 cup vegetable oil

4 eggs

1 1/2 cups all-purpose flour

1/3 cup unsweetened cocoa

1/4 teaspoon salt

2 teaspoons vanilla

3/4 cup chopped nuts

1 (7-oz.) jar marshmallow crème

TOPPING

1/2 cup butter, melted

1/2 cup unsweetened cocoa

1 (16-oz.) pkg. powdered sugar

1/2 cup evaporated milk

1 teaspoon vanilla

3/4 cup chopped nuts

1 Heat oven to 350°F. Spray 13x9-inch pan with nonstick cooking spray.

2 In large bowl, cream sugar and oil. Add eggs and beat at medium speed until light and fluffy. Add flour, 1/3 cup cocoa and salt; beat well. Add 2 teaspoons vanilla, 3/4 cup nuts and marshmallow crème; beat well. Pour mixture into pan.

3 Bake 30 minutes. Cool cake in pan on wire rack until set or about 10 minutes.

4 To prepare topping, combine butter, 1/2 cup cocoa, powdered sugar, evaporated milk, 1 teaspoon vanilla and 3/4 cup chopped nuts in large bowl. Beat at medium speed until smooth. With spatula, spread topping over cake. Store in refrigerator.

16 servings

GREEK NUT CAKE

VASSIE SEMI
LA MESA, CALIFORNIA

CAKE

2 cups buttermilk baking mix

1 cup pecans or walnuts, coarsely chopped

1 cup sugar

1 1/2 teaspoons baking powder

1 teaspoon cinnamon

1/4 teaspoon ground cloves

1/2 teaspoon ground nutmeg

4 eggs

3/4 cup milk

3/4 cup vegetable oil

TOPPING

1 1/2 cups sugar

1 1/4 cups water

2 teaspoons grated orange peel

1 Heat oven to 375°F. Spray 9-inch round cake pan with nonstick cooking spray.

2 In large bowl, stir together baking mix, nuts, 1 cup sugar, baking powder, cinnamon, cloves, nutmeg, eggs, milk and oil until blended. Pour into pan.

3 Bake 30 minutes or until toothpick inserted in center comes out clean.

4 To prepare topping, heat 1 1/2 cups sugar, water and orange peel in medium saucepan over high heat. Bring to a boil. Boil 2 minutes; remove from heat. Let stand until cake is finished baking.

5 Immediately spoon topping over cake. Cool cake in pan on wire rack.

8 servings

HONEY-NUT POUND CAKE

JOHN F. WILLIAMS, SR.
BEAUMONT, TEXAS

1/2 cup butter, softened

1 cup packed brown sugar

2 eggs

2 tablespoons honey

1 1/2 cups cake flour

1/2 teaspoon baking powder

1/4 teaspoon baking soda

1/2 cup buttermilk

2 teaspoons vanilla

1 cup coarsely chopped pecans

1 Heat oven to 350°F. Spray 9x5-inch loaf pan with nonstick cooking spray.

2 In large bowl, beat butter and sugar at medium-high speed until fluffy. Add eggs, one at a time, mixing thoroughly after each addition. Stir in honey.

3 In large bowl, sift together flour, baking powder and baking soda. Gradually add and stir in flour mixture to sugar mixture alternately with buttermilk, ending with buttermilk. Stir in vanilla. Fold 3/4 cup of the chopped pecans into batter. Spoon batter into pan. Sprinkle remaining 1/4 cup pecans on top.

4 Bake 50 to 55 minutes or until toothpick inserted in center comes out clean. Cool in pan on wire rack. Store in refrigerator.

12 servings

CHOCOLATE-CHERRY CAKE

DOROTHY H. JOHNSON
HECTOR, MINNESOTA

CAKE

2/3 cup butter

2 cups sugar

2 eggs

2 (1-oz.) squares unsweetened chocolate, melted

2 cups all-purpose flour

2 teaspoons baking soda

1 teaspoon salt

1 (8-oz.) jar maraschino cherries, drained, juice reserved, cut up

Buttermilk to make 2 cups liquid

ICING

6 tablespoons butter

6 tablespoons milk

1 1/2 cups sugar

1 teaspoon vanilla

1/2 cup semisweet chocolate chips

1 Heat oven to 350°F. Spray 13x9-inch pan with nonstick cooking spray.

2 In large bowl, beat 2/3 cup butter and 2 cups sugar at medium-high speed until fluffy. Add eggs and chocolate; beat well.

3 In another large bowl, mix together flour, baking soda and salt. To reserved cherry juice, add enough buttermilk to make 2 cups. Add buttermilk mixture alternately with flour to batter, mixing well. Fold in cherries. Pour into pan.

4 Bake 1 hour or until toothpick inserted in center comes out clean. Cool cake in pan on wire rack.

5 To prepare icing, in large saucepan, heat remaining 6 tablespoons butter, milk and 1 1/2 cups sugar to a boil; boil 30 seconds. Remove from heat; add vanilla and chocolate chips. Beat by hand 3 minutes. Spread icing over cooled cake.

8 servings

TEXAS SHEET CAKE

KITTI BOESEL
GLEN BURNIE, MARYLAND

$\frac{1}{2}$ cup unsweetened cocoa

$1\frac{1}{2}$ cups butter

1 cup water

2 cups sugar

2 cups all-purpose flour

$\frac{1}{2}$ teaspoon salt

1 cup sour cream

1 teaspoon baking soda

2 eggs

2 teaspoons vanilla

1 teaspoon cinnamon

6 tablespoons milk

1 (16-oz.) pkg. powdered sugar

1 Heat oven to 375°F. Spray 15$\frac{1}{2}$x10$\frac{1}{2}$x1-inch baking pan with nonstick cooking spray.

2 Heat $\frac{1}{4}$ cup of the cocoa, 1 cup of the butter, and water to boiling in small saucepan over high heat; remove from heat. Stir in sugar, flour and salt. Beat in sour cream, baking soda, eggs, 1 teaspoon of the vanilla and cinnamon at medium speed 1 minute or until blended, scraping bowl occasionally. Pour into pan.

3 Bake 20 minutes or until toothpick inserted in center comes out clean.

4 Meanwhile, beat remaining $\frac{1}{4}$ cup cocoa, remaining $\frac{1}{2}$ cup butter, milk, powdered sugar and remaining 1 teaspoon vanilla until smooth.

5 Pour sugar mixture over warm cake. Sprinkle with nuts or coconut, if desired. Cool cake in pan on wire rack.

20 servings

LEMON POPPY SEED CAKE

BETTY BARRETT
OAKHURST, CALIFORNIA

$1\frac{1}{4}$ cups all-purpose flour

$\frac{2}{3}$ cup sugar

$\frac{1}{2}$ cup cornstarch

1 tablespoon poppy seeds

$2\frac{1}{4}$ teaspoons baking powder

1 teaspoon salt

2 tablespoons butter

1 cup skim milk

2 teaspoons freshly grated lemon peel

$1\frac{1}{2}$ teaspoons vanilla

1 egg

1 Heat oven to 350°F. Spray 8-inch round cake pan with nonstick cooking spray; lightly flour.

2 In large bowl, whisk together flour, sugar, cornstarch, poppy seeds, baking powder and salt. Blend in butter with fingers until incorporated.

3 In large measuring cup or bowl, lightly beat together milk, lemon peel, vanilla and egg. Stir milk mixture into flour mixture until just blended. Pour batter into pan.

4 Bake 35 minutes or until toothpick inserted in center comes out clean. Cool in pan 10 minutes on wire rack. Remove from pan; cool completely.

8 servings

WACKY CAKE WITH CARAMEL ICING

WACKY CAKE WITH CARAMEL ICING

LEEANN WHEELER
GRANTS, NEW MEXICO

CAKE

3 cups all-purpose flour

2 cups sugar

2 cups cold water

1$\frac{1}{2}$ cups oil

6 tablespoons unsweetened cocoa*

1 teaspoon salt

2 tablespoons apple cider vinegar

2 teaspoons vanilla

2 teaspoons soda water

ICING

2 tablespoons butter

$\frac{1}{2}$ cup packed brown sugar

3 tablespoons milk

$\frac{3}{4}$ cup sugar

1 Heat oven to 350°F. Spray 13x9-inch pan with nonstick cooking spray.

2 In large bowl, combine flour, sugar, water, oil, cocoa, salt, vinegar, vanilla and soda water; mix thoroughly. Pour into pan.

3 Bake 30 to 40 minutes or until toothpick inserted in center comes out clean. Cool in pan on wire rack.

4 To prepare icing, melt butter in small saucepan over medium heat. Stir in brown sugar. Cook, stirring constantly, until sugar melts and mixture is bubbly. Remove from heat. Cool 5 minutes. Stir in milk. Beat in sugar at low speed 1 minute. Beat at medium speed another minute or until frosting is smooth. Spread over cake.

TIP *For an easy and delicious white cake, omit unsweetened cocoa.

16 servings

CHOCOLATE-ZUCCHINI CAKE

CHRIS McBEE
XENIA, OHIO

2 cups all-purpose flour

1 teaspoon baking powder

1 teaspoon baking soda

$\frac{1}{2}$ teaspoon salt

1 teaspoon cinnamon

$\frac{1}{4}$ cup unsweetened cocoa

3 eggs

1$\frac{1}{2}$ cups sugar

$\frac{1}{2}$ cup vegetable oil

$\frac{3}{4}$ cup buttermilk

2 medium zucchini, coarsely shredded

1 teaspoon vanilla

1 cup coarsely chopped walnuts

$\frac{1}{2}$ cup raisins

1 tablespoon powdered sugar

1 Heat oven to 350°F. Spray 10-cup Bundt pan with nonstick cooking spray.

2 In large bowl, combine flour, baking powder, baking soda, salt, cinnamon and cocoa; mix well. Set aside.

3 In another large bowl, beat eggs at high speed until light and fluffy. Gradually beat in sugar. In medium bowl, stir together vegetable oil, buttermilk and zucchini. Gradually add and stir in zucchini mixture alternately with dry ingredients. Stir in vanilla, walnuts and raisins at low speed. Pour into pan.

4 Bake 55 to 60 minutes or until toothpick inserted in center comes out clean. Cool in pan on wire rack 10 minutes; invert cake and cool completely. Just before serving, sift powdered sugar over cake.

12 servings

MELT-IN-YOUR-MOUTH BLUEBERRY CAKE

STEPHANIE WICKE
VALPARAISO, INDIANA

2 eggs, separated

1 cup sugar plus 2 tablespoons

1/2 cup butter

1/2 teaspoon salt

1 teaspoon vanilla

1 1/2 cups all-purpose flour

1 teaspoon baking powder

1/3 cup milk

1 1/2 cups blueberries, dusted with flour

1 teaspoon cinnamon

1 Heat oven to 350°F. Spray 8-inch square pan with nonstick cooking spray.

2 In large bowl, beat egg whites at medium speed until foamy; beat in 1/4 cup of the sugar. Continue beating until stiff peaks form.

3 In another large bowl, beat butter, salt, vanilla, 3/4 cup sugar and egg yolks until light and creamy.

4 In another bowl, sift together flour and baking powder. Stir gradually into batter, alternating with milk. Fold in egg whites and blueberries. Spoon into pan. Combine remaining 2 tablespoons sugar and cinnamon; sprinkle over batter.

5 Bake 50 minutes or until toothpick inserted in center comes out clean. Cool cake in pan on wire rack.

9 servings

APPLESAUCE SPICE CAKE WITH PENUCHE FROSTING

RHONDA HARRELL
CHINO HILLS, CALIFORNIA

CAKE

1/2 cup shortening

2 1/2 cups all-purpose flour

2 cups sugar

3/4 teaspoon salt

3/4 teaspoon baking soda

1/4 teaspoon baking powder

1 teaspoon cinnamon

1/2 teaspoon allspice

1/2 teaspoon ground cloves

3/4 teaspoon nutmeg

1/2 cup milk

2 eggs

2 cups applesauce

FROSTING

1/2 cup butter

1 cup packed brown sugar

1 teaspoon vanilla

1/4 cup milk

3 cups powdered sugar

1 Heat oven to 350°F. Spray 13x9-inch pan with nonstick cooking spray.

2 In large bowl, beat together shortening and flour at medium speed. In medium bowl, mix together sugar, salt, baking soda, baking powder, cinnamon, allspice, cloves and nutmeg. Stir into shortening mixture gradually. Add 1/2 cup milk, eggs and applesauce; mix thoroughly at medium speed. Pour into pan.

3 Bake 45 to 50 minutes or until toothpick inserted in center comes out clean. Cool cake in pan on wire rack.

4 To prepare frosting, melt butter in small saucepan over medium heat; stir in brown sugar. Cook until bubbly. Add vanilla, stir and remove from heat. Add 1/4 cup milk; beat vigorously by hand until smooth. Beat in enough powdered sugar for smooth frosting. Frost cake quickly.

12 servings

JUNIE'S PINEAPPLE CAKE

PEGGY WINKWORTH
DURANGO, COLORADO

CAKE

2 cups sugar

2 cups all-purpose flour

2 teaspoons baking soda

2 eggs, slightly beaten

1 (20-oz.) can crushed pineapple with juice

1 cup chopped walnuts

FROSTING

1 (8-oz.) pkg. cream cheese, softened

$\frac{1}{2}$ cup butter, softened

2 cups powdered sugar

1 teaspoon vanilla

1 Heat oven to 350°F. Spray 13x9-inch pan with nonstick cooking spray.

2 In large bowl, stir together sugar, flour, baking soda, eggs, pineapple and $\frac{3}{4}$ cup of the walnuts. Pour mixture into pan.

3 Bake 30 to 45 minutes or until toothpick inserted in center comes out clean. Cool cake in pan on wire rack.

4 To prepare frosting, beat cream cheese, butter, powdered sugar and vanilla at medium speed in large bowl until frosting is smooth. Frost cake while slightly warm. Sprinkle with remaining $\frac{1}{4}$ cup walnuts. Store in refrigerator.

16 servings

COCONUT BREAD

DOROTHY H. JOHNSON
HECTOR, MINNESOTA

BREAD

4 eggs

2 cups sugar

1 cup vegetable oil

2 teaspoons coconut extract

3 cups all-purpose flour

$\frac{1}{2}$ teaspoon baking powder

$\frac{1}{2}$ teaspoon baking soda

1 cup buttermilk

1 cup coconut

1 cup nuts, if desired

GLAZE

$1\frac{1}{2}$ cups sugar

3 tablespoons butter

$\frac{3}{4}$ cup water

1 teaspoon coconut extract

1 Heat oven to 325°F. Spray 2 (9x5-inch) loaf pans with nonstick cooking spray, lightly flour.

2 In large bowl, combine eggs, 2 cups sugar, oil and 2 teaspoons coconut extract. Gradually add and stir in flour, baking powder and baking soda alternately with buttermilk. Stir in coconut and nuts. Pour mixture into pans.

3 Bake 1 hour or until toothpick inserted in center comes out clean. Cool slightly in pans on wire rack; remove from pans.

4 To prepare glaze, combine $1\frac{1}{2}$ cups sugar, butter, water and 1 teaspoon coconut extract in medium saucepan. Heat to boiling; cook 5 minutes, stirring occasionally. Pour over warm breads. Let stand 3 to 4 hours. Store in refrigerator.

2 loaves

OLD-FASHIONED APPLESAUCE CAKE

STEPHANIE BAKER
HAMDEN, OHIO

1/2 cup butter

2 cups sugar

3 eggs

3 cups all-purpose flour

2 teaspoons baking soda

1 teaspoon salt

2 tablespoons cinnamon

1/2 teaspoon ground nutmeg

1/2 teaspoon allspice

2 cups applesauce

1 cup raisins

3/4 cup chopped walnuts

1 Heat oven to 350°F. Spray 13x9-inch pan with nonstick cooking spray.

2 In large bowl, beat butter, sugar and eggs at medium-high speed until light and fluffy. In another large bowl, sift together flour, baking soda, salt, cinnamon, nutmeg and allspice. Stir flour mixture gradually in butter mixture, alternating with applesauce. Stir in raisins and nuts. Pour into pan.

3 Bake 50 to 60 minutes or until toothpick inserted in center comes out clean. Cool in pan on wire rack. Sprinkle with powdered sugar or top with cream cheese icing, if desired.

12 servings

BLUEBERRY TEA CAKE WITH LEMON SAUCE

KIM KOPPLIN
GRAND JUNCTION, COLORADO

CAKE

2 cups all-purpose flour

1 cup sugar

2 teaspoons baking powder

1/4 teaspoon salt

1/3 cup shortening

3/4 cup milk

1 egg

1 cup rinsed fresh blueberries

SAUCE

1/4 cup sugar

1 teaspoon cornstarch

3 teaspoons lemon juice

1 cup water

1 teaspoon grated lemon peel

1 teaspoon butter

1 Heat oven to 350°F. Spray 8-inch square pan with nonstick cooking spray.

2 In large bowl, combine flour, 1 cup sugar, baking powder and 1/4 teaspoon salt; mix in shortening. Add milk; beat vigorously by hand 2 minutes. Add egg and beat an additional 1 minute. Carefully fold in blueberries. Pour into pan.

3 Bake 50 minutes or until toothpick inserted in center comes out clean. Cool 30 minutes in pan on wire rack.

4 To prepare sauce, stir together 1/4 cup sugar, cornstarch, lemon juice and water in medium saucepan. Stir until smooth. Add lemon peel. Cook over medium heat until mixture thickens and becomes clear, stirring frequently. Remove from heat. Add butter; stir until butter is melted and well incorporated. Spread over cake.

9 servings

**BLUEBERRY TEA CAKE
WITH LEMON SAUCE**

COMPANY CRANBERRY TEA CAKE

GWEN CAMPBELL
STERLING, VIRGINIA

1 cup fresh cranberries, halved

¾ cup sugar

1 egg

2 cups all-purpose flour

2 teaspoons baking powder

1 teaspoon ground allspice

¼ teaspoon salt

⅓ cup milk

3 tablespoons butter, softened

1 teaspoon vanilla

¾ cup toasted almonds, coursely chopped

1 Heat oven to 350°F. Spray 11x7-inch pan with nonstick cooking spray.

2 In large bowl, combine cranberries with 2 tablespoons of the sugar; set aside. In medium bowl, beat egg; gradually beat in ½ cup sugar.

3 Sift together flour, baking powder, allspice and salt. Add to egg mixture alternately with milk, mixing well. Add butter and vanilla; beat thoroughly. Fold in cranberries and almonds. Pour mixture into pan; sprinkle with remaining 2 tablespoons sugar.

4 Bake 30 minutes or until toothpick inserted in center comes out clean. Cool in pan on wire rack. Serve warm or at room temperature.

12 servings

FRESH APPLE CAKE

ARTIS OLSON
GRANITE FALLS, MINNESOTA

CAKE

¼ cup butter

1 cup sugar

1 egg

1 cup all-purpose flour

1 teaspoon baking soda

½ teaspoon cinnamon

½ teaspoon salt

2 cups chopped apples

½ cup chopped walnuts

SAUCE

¼ cup butter

¼ cup half-and-half

¼ cup sugar

¼ cup packed brown sugar

1 teaspoon all-purpose flour

1 teaspoon vanilla

1 Heat oven to 350°F. Spray 9-inch round cake pan with nonstick cooking spray.

2 Beat ¼ cup butter and 1 cup sugar at medium speed until light and fluffy. Add egg; mix well. Stir together 1 cup flour, baking soda, cinnamon and salt; add to butter mixture. Fold in apples; spoon into prepared pan. Sprinkle walnuts on top of mixture.

3 Bake 40 to 45 minutes or until toothpick inserted into center comes out clean. Cool in pan on wire rack.

4 To prepare sauce, heat ¼ cup butter, half-and-half, ¼ cup sugar, brown sugar and 1 teaspoon flour in heavy saucepan. Bring to a boil; cook until sugars are dissolved. Add vanilla. Spread on cake.

9 servings

SAUCEPAN RAISIN SPICE CAKE WITH CARAMEL FROSTING

LENA RICE
BOISE, IDAHO

CAKE

1 cup raisins

2 cups water

$1/2$ cup shortening

1 cup sugar

$1^3/4$ cups all-purpose flour

1 teaspoon baking soda

1 teaspoon cinnamon

1 teaspoon ground cloves

1 teaspoon ground nutmeg

$1/2$ cup chopped nuts

FROSTING

$1/4$ cup butter

$1/2$ cup packed brown sugar

3 tablespoons milk

$1/2$ teaspoon vanilla

2 cups powdered sugar

1 Heat oven to 350°F. Spray 3-quart casserole with nonstick cooking spray.

2 In large saucepan, simmer raisins in water 10 minutes; remove from heat. While still warm, add shortening and sugar. Cool 5 minutes. Add flour, baking soda, cinnamon, cloves, nutmeg and nuts; mix well. Pour into baking dish.

3 Bake 35 to 40 minutes or until toothpick inserted in center comes out clean. Cool in pan on wire rack.

4 To prepare frosting, melt butter in medium saucepan over low heat. Add brown sugar; cook until blended and hot. Add milk; bring to a boil. Boil 30 seconds. Remove from heat; beat in vanilla and enough powdered sugar for a smooth frosting.

12 servings

AUNT GRACE'S BANANA BREAD

CARLENE S. GOODEILL
CHICO, CALIFORNIA

$3/4$ cup butter

$1^1/2$ cups sugar

$1^1/2$ cups mashed bananas

2 eggs, beaten

1 teaspoon vanilla

2 cups all-purpose flour

1 teaspoon baking soda

$3/4$ teaspoon salt

$2/3$ cup buttermilk*

$3/4$ cup walnuts, chopped

1 Heat oven to 325°F. Spray 2 ($8^1/2$ x$4^1/2$ x$2^1/2$-inch) loaf pans with nonstick cooking spray.

2 In large bowl, beat butter and sugar at medium speed until smooth. Stir in bananas, eggs and vanilla. In another bowl, mix together flour, baking soda and salt; stir into banana mixture alternately with buttermilk. Fold in nuts.

3 Bake 1 hour and 15 minutes or until toothpick inserted in center comes out clean. Cool in pans on wire rack. Remove from pans. Store in refrigerator.

TIP *To substitute for buttermilk, use 2 teaspoons lemon juice plus regular milk to make ⅔ cup.

2 loaves

BUTTERSCOTCH PECANNANA BREAD
ZUCCHINI-PISTACHIO BREAD

BUTTERSCOTCH PECANNANA BREAD

GWEN CAMPBELL
STERLING, VIRGINIA

3 1/2 cups all-purpose flour

4 teaspoons baking powder

1 teaspoon baking soda

1 teaspoon cinnamon

1 teaspoon nutmeg

1/4 teaspoon mace

1 teaspoon salt

2 1/4 cups mashed ripe bananas

1 1/2 cups packed brown sugar

2 eggs

1/2 cup melted butter

1/2 cup milk

3 cups chopped pecans

2 cups butterscotch or semisweet chocolate chips (12 oz.)

1 Heat oven to 350°F. Spray 2 (9x5-inch) loaf pans with nonstick cooking spray.

2 In large bowl, combine flour, baking powder, baking soda, cinnamon, nutmeg, mace and salt; set aside. In another bowl, combine bananas, brown sugar, eggs and butter; beat at medium speed until smooth. Gradually add flour mixture alternately with milk to banana mixture; blend well. Stir in 2 cups of the pecans and butterscotch chips. Pour mixture into pans; sprinkle with remaining 1 cup pecans.

3 Bake 60 to 70 minutes or until toothpick inserted in center comes out clean. Cool in pans on wire rack; remove from pans. Store in refrigerator.

2 loaves

ZUCCHINI-PISTACHIO BREAD

CHERYL PETERSON

BREAD

1 1/2 cups all-purpose flour

1 1/2 teaspoons baking soda

1/4 teaspoon cinnamon

3/4 cup sugar

2 eggs

1/2 cup vegetable oil

1 teaspoon vanilla

1/2 teaspoon salt

1 1/2 cups grated zucchini, squeezed dry

1 1/2 cups toasted shelled pistachios, coarsely chopped

FROSTING

1 pasteurized egg white

3/4 cup sugar

2 1/2 tablespoons cold water

1/8 teaspoon cream of tartar

3/4 teaspoon light corn syrup

1/2 teaspoon vanilla

1 Heat oven to 350°F. Spray 9x5-inch loaf pan with nonstick cooking spray.

2 In large bowl, mix together flour, baking soda and cinnamon. In another bowl, whisk together 3/4 cup sugar, eggs, oil, 1 teaspoon vanilla and salt. Add to flour mixture; stir until combined. Fold in zucchini and nuts. Spoon batter into pan.

3 Bake 50 to 60 minutes or until toothpick inserted into center comes out clean. Cool in pan on wire rack. Remove from pan.

4 To prepare frosting, combine egg white, 3/4 cup sugar, water, cream of tartar and corn syrup in double boiler over simmering water. Using hand mixer, beat mixture 7 minutes or until thick and fluffy. Beat in 1/2 teaspoon vanilla. Spread over loaf. Store in refrigerator.

1 loaf

HAWAIIAN REGENT MANGO BREAD

DOLORES NELSON
ROSEBURG, OREGON

1 cup vegetable oil

3/4 cup sugar

3 eggs

2 cups all-purpose flour

2 teaspoons baking powder

1/2 teaspoon cinnamon

1/2 teaspoon ground nutmeg

2 cups chopped fresh mango

1/4 cup macadamia nuts

1/4 cup chopped dates

1/4 cup raisins

1 Heat oven to 350°F. Spray 1 (81/2 x41/2 x21/2-inch) loaf pan with nonstick cooking spray.

2 In large bowl, beat oil, sugar and eggs at medium speed until smooth. Stir in flour, baking powder, cinnamon and nutmeg just until moistened. Stir in mango, nuts, dates and raisins. Pour into pan.

3 Bake 1 hour or until toothpick inserted in center comes out clean. Cool in pan on wire rack. Remove from pan. Store in refrigerator.

1 loaf

PAM'S GRAND PRIZE-WINNING ZUCCHINI-BUTTERSCOTCH NUT BREAD

PAM MILLIGAN
ARROYO GRANDE, CALIFORNIA

3 ripe bananas, mashed

2 cups packed brown sugar

31/2 cups all-purpose flour

2 teaspoons baking soda

1/2 teaspoon baking powder

1 teaspoon salt

3 eggs

1 cup vegetable oil

1 tablespoon vanilla

1 (15-oz.) can cream of coconut*

2 cups grated zucchini

11/2 cups chopped walnuts

1 cup butterscotch chips (6 oz.)

1 Heat oven to 350°F. Spray 2 (81/2 x41/2 x21/2-inch) loaf pans with nonstick cooking spray.

2 In large bowl, beat bananas and brown sugar at low speed until combined. In separate bowl, combine flour, baking soda, baking powder and salt.

3 In another large bowl, beat eggs at medium speed. Beat in oil, vanilla, cream of coconut and banana mixture. Add flour mixture, zucchini, walnuts and butterscotch chips; beat well. Spoon mixture into pans.

4 Bake 45 to 60 minutes or until toothpick inserted in center comes out clean. Cool slightly in pans on wire racks; remove from pans. Serve warm slices with one scoop vanilla ice cream drizzled with caramel sauce, if desired. Store in refrigerator.

TIP *Cream of coconut can be found in liquor stores.

2 loaves

CARROT BREAD

JUNE POEPPING
QUINCY, ILLINOIS

BREAD

1 cup vegetable oil

3/4 cup sugar

2 eggs

1 teaspoon vanilla

1 1/2 cups all-purpose flour

1 1/2 teaspoons baking soda

1 1/2 teaspoons cinnamon

1/2 teaspoon salt

1 1/2 cups shredded carrots

1 1/2 cups chopped nuts

GLAZE

1/2 cup powdered sugar

1 teaspoon grated lemon peel

1 tablespoon lemon juice

1 Heat oven to 350°F. Spray 9x5-inch loaf pan with nonstick cooking spray.

2 In large bowl, combine oil, sugar, eggs and vanilla. In separate bowl, combine flour, baking soda, cinnamon and salt. Add to oil mixture; mix just until moistened. Stir in carrots and nuts. Pour mixture into pan.

3 Bake 60 to 70 minutes or until toothpick inserted in center comes out clean. Cool in pan on wire rack 10 minutes. Remove from pan; let cool completely.

4 Meanwhile, mix powdered sugar, lemon peel and juice. Drizzle over top of cooled bread. Store in refrigerator.

1 loaf

STRAWBERRY NICE BREAD

HERMAN STAHL
JOHNSON CITY, NEW YORK

1 3/4 cups all-purpose flour

2 teaspoons baking powder

1/4 teaspoon baking soda

1/8 teaspoon salt

2 eggs, beaten

1/2 cup sugar

1/3 cup vegetable oil

1/2 cup mashed fresh strawberries

1/2 cup strawberry preserves

1/4 cup chopped walnuts

1 Heat oven to 350°F. Spray 9x5-inch loaf pan with nonstick cooking spray.

2 In large bowl, mix together flour, baking powder, baking soda and salt. In another bowl, combine eggs, sugar and oil. Add to flour mixture; mix well. Stir in strawberries, preserves and walnuts. Spoon mixture into pan.

3 Bake 50 minutes or until toothpick inserted in center comes out clean. Cool in pan on wire rack. Remove from pan. Store in refrigerator.

1 loaf

PIES, CRISPS &

FRUIT COBBLERS

AUTUMN CARAMEL APPLE PIE (page 40)

SOUR CREAM PIE SHELL

CHARLOTTE WARD
HILTON HEAD, SOUTH CAROLINA

1/4 cup plus 2 tablespoons sour cream

2 tablespoons ice water

1 teaspoon sugar

3/4 teaspoon salt

2 1/2 cups all-purpose flour

1/2 cup butter, chilled, cut up

1/2 cup shortening, chilled

1 In small bowl, combine sour cream, ice water, sugar and salt. In large bowl, combine flour, butter and shortening with fingers or pastry blender until mixture crumbles. Add sour cream mixture; stir together just until dough forms.

2 Turn dough out onto lightly floured surface; divide in half. Form each half into ball; flatten into 6-inch disk. Wrap each disk in resealable plastic bag; refrigerate 1 hour.

3 Roll crust 1/8 inch thick; press into 2 (9-inch) pie pans. Refrigerate 30 minutes before adding filling of your choice. If baking without filling, refrigerate 45 minutes to 1 hour. Store in refrigerator.

2 (9-inch) pie shells

PINA COLADA PIE

BRISBIN FAMILY
BAY CITY, MICHIGAN

CRUST

2 cups crushed graham crackers

1/2 cup coconut, toasted

1/2 cup melted butter

FILLING

1/4 cup cornstarch

2/3 cup sugar

1/4 teaspoon salt

3 cups cream

3 egg yolks, slightly beaten

1/2 teaspoon vanilla

2 tablespoons butter

1 cup shredded coconut

1/2 cup crushed pineapple, well drained

TOPPING

3 egg whites

1/4 teaspoon cream of tartar

6 tablespoons sugar

1/4 cup toasted coconut

Maraschino cherries

1 Heat oven to 400°F.

2 In 9-inch pie pan, combine crackers, 1/2 cup coconut and 1/2 cup butter. Press firmly and evenly against sides and bottom. Refrigerate 1 hour or until firm.

3 To prepare filling, combine cornstarch, 2/3 cup sugar and salt in medium saucepan. Slowly whisk in cream. Bring to a boil over medium heat, stirring constantly. In small bowl, add 1/2 cup hot cream mixture to egg yolks. Whisk together; pour back into saucepan. Cook 5 minutes, stirring constantly, until thickened. Remove from heat.

4 Add vanilla, 2 tablespoons butter, 1 cup coconut and pineapple; mix well. Cool slightly; pour into crust. Refrigerate.

5 To prepare topping, combine egg whites and cream of tartar in large bowl. Beat at medium speed until frothy. Increase speed to medium-high. Add 6 tablespoons sugar, 1 tablespoon at a time, until sugar is dissolved and stiff peaks form. Spread topping over pie; form peaks with back of spoon. Top with 1/4 cup toasted coconut. Bake 8 minutes or until top is slightly browned. Refrigerate at least 3 hours. Garnish with cherries. Store in refrigerator.

10 servings

MOM'S CHERRY CRUNCH DESSERT

PEGGY WINKWORTH
DURANGO, COLORADO

1 1/2 cups all-purpose flour

3/4 cup old-fashioned or quick-cooking oats

1 cup packed brown sugar

1/2 teaspoon baking soda

1/2 teaspoon salt

1/2 cup butter, softened

1 (22-oz.) can cherry pie filling

1 Heat oven to 350°F.

2 In medium bowl, combine flour, oats, brown sugar, baking soda and salt. Cut in butter using two knives or pastry blender until mixture crumbles.

3 Press one-half of mixture into ungreased 9-inch square pan. Pour pie filling into pie shell; sprinkle remaining crumbly mixture over pie filling.

4 Bake 40 to 50 minutes or until lightly browned. Cool on wire rack.

8 servings

UPSIDE-DOWN CARAMEL APPLE PIE

CLAUDIA WENDEL
FRESNO, CALIFORNIA

3 tablespoons butter, softened

1 (15-oz.) pkg. refrigerated pie crusts

1 1/2 cups pecan halves

1/2 cup packed brown sugar

1 cup sugar

2 tablespoons all-purpose flour

1/4 teaspoon salt

1/2 teaspoon cinnamon

1/4 teaspoon nutmeg

1/8 teaspoon allspice

5 cups peeled sliced apples

1 Heat oven to 450°F. Line 9-inch pie pan with 14-inch circle of aluminum foil. Spread 2 tablespoons of the butter over bottom and sides of aluminum foil.

2 Press pecan halves into butter around sides and bottom of pan. Sprinkle with brown sugar. Spray edges of pan with nonstick cooking spray.

3 Place one pie crust over pecans; press evenly. In large bowl, stir together sugar, flour, salt, cinnamon, nutmeg and allspice. Toss apples in flour mixture; spoon into pastry in plate. Dot with remaining 1 tablespoon butter. Cover with second pie crust; crimp edges. Cut two or three slits in top crust.

4 Bake 10 minutes. Reduce oven temperature to 375°F. Bake an additional 35 to 40 minutes or until pastry is golden brown. Remove from oven and cool 5 minutes. Invert onto serving plate. Serve warm.

8 servings

DELUXE CHOCOLATE CREAM
PIE WITH MERINGUE

DELUXE CHOCOLATE CREAM PIE WITH MERINGUE

MRS. FAYNELL BEAVER
LANDIS, NORTH CAROLINA

2 (1-oz.) squares unsweetened chocolate

1 cup plus 6 tablespoons sugar

1/4 teaspoon salt

3 tablespoons cornstarch

3 eggs, separated

2 1/2 cups milk, warm

2 tablespoons butter

1/2 teaspoon vanilla

1 (9-inch) baked pie shell

1 Heat oven to 350°F.

2 In medium saucepan, melt chocolate over low heat. In small bowl, combine 1 cup of the sugar, salt and cornstarch; stir into chocolate. Stir in egg yolks and milk. Cook over medium heat until thickened, stirring constantly. Remove from heat; stir in butter and vanilla. Pour into pie shell; set aside.

3 To prepare meringue, beat egg whites at medium speed until foamy. Beat in remaining 6 tablespoons of the sugar, 1 tablespoon at a time; continue to beat until stiff and glossy. Spread meringue over pie, making sure meringue is touching crust around entire edge. Bake 12 to 15 minutes or until meringue is lightly browned. Cool on wire rack. Store in refrigerator.

8 servings

PECAN PIE IN SPICY PECAN CRUST

AMY SMOUSE
CORTEZ, COLORADO

FILLING

3 eggs

1 cup corn syrup

1/2 cup packed brown sugar

1/4 cup sugar

1/3 cup melted butter

1 tablespoon brandy

1/2 teaspoon vanilla

1 1/2 cups pecan halves

CRUST

1 cup all-purpose flour

1/4 cup ground pecans

1 teaspoon cinnamon

1 teaspoon nutmeg

1/4 teaspoon salt

1/3 cup shortening

1/2 teaspoon brandy

2 to 4 tablespoons cold water

1 Heat oven to 350°F.

2 For filling, beat eggs at medium speed in large bowl. Stir in corn syrup, brown sugar, sugar, butter, 1 tablespoon brandy and vanilla. Stir in 1 1/2 cups pecans. Set aside.

3 For crust, stir together flour, 1/4 cup pecans, cinnamon, nutmeg and salt in medium bowl. Cut in shortening with two knives or pastry blender until mixture crumbles. Sprinkle 1/2 teaspoon brandy over mixture; blend with fork. Sprinkle in water, 1 teaspoon at a time, just until dough forms a ball. Refrigerate 15 minutes.

4 On floured surface, roll dough into 12-inch circle; press into 9-inch pie pan. Flute edges. Pour filling into crust; cover edges with aluminum foil and bake 25 minutes. Remove aluminum foil and bake an additional 30 minutes or until lightly browned. Cool on wire rack. Store in refrigerator.

8 servings

COUNTRY RHUBARB PIE

FANNIE LINE
MILLERSBURG, OHIO

FILLING

1 egg

1 teaspoon vanilla

1 cup sugar

1 tablespoon all-purpose flour

$1/2$ teaspoon cinnamon

$1/4$ teaspoon freshly grated nutmeg

3 cups sliced ($1/2$-inch thick) rhubarb

1 (9-inch) unbaked pie shell

TOPPING

$1/2$ cup butter, softened

$1/2$ cup all-purpose flour

$1/4$ cup packed brown sugar

$1/4$ cup sugar

$1/4$ cup chopped walnuts

2 tablespoons old-fashioned or quick-cooking oats

1 Heat oven to 400°F.

2 In large bowl, beat eggs slightly; add vanilla. In another bowl, stir together 1 cup sugar, 1 tablespoon flour, cinnamon and nutmeg; add to egg mixture. Add rhubarb; pour into pie shell. Stir together butter, $1/2$ cup flour, brown sugar, $1/4$ cup sugar, walnuts and oats until crumbly; sprinkle over rhubarb.

3 Bake 10 minutes. Reduce oven temperature to 350°F; bake an additional 40 minutes or until crust is golden brown. Cool on wire rack. Store in refrigerator.

8 servings

WILMA SHORTCAKE

KAY SPARKMAN
ALEXANDRIA, VIRGINIA

3 cups all-purpose flour

$4 1/2$ teaspoons baking powder

$1 1/2$ teaspoons salt

5 tablespoons sugar

$3/4$ cup butter

2 eggs, slightly beaten

$1/2$ cup milk

1 Heat oven to 400°F.

2 In large bowl, whisk together flour, baking powder, salt and sugar. Cut in butter using two knives or pastry blender until mixture crumbles. Add eggs and milk; mix thoroughly.

3 Shape dough into individual cakes about 3 inches in diameter; place in 13x9-inch pan. Bake 15 minutes or until golden brown. Serve warm with sliced fruit and whipped cream or ice cream, if desired.

12 servings

BLACKBERRY COBBLER

TAMMY RAYNES
NATCHITOCHES, LOUISIANA

$1/2$ cup melted butter

1 cup all-purpose flour

$1 1/2$ teaspoons baking powder

$1/8$ teaspoon salt

1 cup sugar

$3/4$ cup milk

1 teaspoon vanilla

4 cups fresh blackberries or 2 (10-oz.) pkg. frozen blackberries, thawed

1 Heat oven to 375°F.

2 Pour butter into 2-quart casserole; set aside. In large bowl, combine flour, baking powder, salt and sugar; stir well. Add milk, vanilla and blackberries to flour mixture; stir until well blended. Spoon batter into casserole (do not stir).

3 Bake, uncovered, 40 to 45 minutes or until golden brown. Serve warm. Store in refrigerator.

6 servings

PEACH PIE

THERESA GAUDETTE
NORTH NEW PORTLAND, MAINE

2 (9-inch) unbaked pie shells

3 cups sliced fresh peaches

1 cup sugar

3 tablespoons all-purpose flour

3 tablespoons butter

1/4 teaspoon nutmeg

1/4 teaspoon cinnamon

1 Heat oven to 400°F.

2 Place 1 pie shell in 9-inch pie pan. In medium bowl, combine peaches, sugar, flour, 2 tablespoons of the butter, nutmeg and cinnamon; pour into crust. Dot with remaining 1 tablespoon butter. Top with remaining pastry; crimp edges.

3 Bake 45 to 50 minutes or until crust is golden brown. Cool on wire rack. Serve warm or cool with ice cream or whipped cream, if desired.

8 servings

CHESS PIES

SANDRA K. SNETHEN
MINNEAPOLIS, MINNESOTA

1/2 cup butter

1 cup sugar

2 eggs

1 cup raisins or chopped dates

1 cup finely chopped walnuts

1 teaspoon vanilla

1 (15-oz.) pkg. refrigerated pie crusts

1 Heat oven to 350°F.

2 In large bowl, beat together butter and sugar at high speed until fluffy. Beat in eggs. Stir in raisins, walnuts and vanilla.

3 Unfold pie crusts. Using 3 1/2-inch round cutter, cut 12 circles from pie crust rounds. Place pie crust circles in each of 12 regular-size muffin cups, pressing into bottoms and up sides of cups. Divide filling evenly among cups.

4 Bake 25 to 30 minutes or until set. Cool on wire rack. Store in refrigerator.

12 servings

JEN'S CRUMBLY APPLE PIE

JENNIFER GULLO
RENO, NEVADA

CRUST

1 cup all-purpose flour

1/2 teaspoon salt

1/3 cup shortening, chilled

1/4 cup ice water

FILLING

7 Granny Smith apples, peeled, cored, very thinly sliced

1/2 cup sugar

1 teaspoon cinnamon

1/4 teaspoon nutmeg

1/4 teaspoon salt

TOPPING

3/4 cup packed brown sugar

3/4 cup all-purpose flour

1/2 teaspoon nutmeg

1/3 cup butter, chilled, cut into small pieces

1 Place oven rack in lowest position. Heat oven to 400°F.

2 To prepare crust, stir together 1 cup flour and 1/2 teaspoon salt in medium bowl. Using 2 knives or pastry blender, cut shortening into flour mixture until mixture crumbles. Add ice water, 1 teaspoon at a time, tossing with fork, until dough forms. Shape into 8-inch disk; wrap in plastic wrap. Refrigerate 30 minutes.

3 On floured work surface, using floured rolling pin, roll dough into 12-inch circle. Press into 9-inch pie pan. Trim excess dough, leaving 1-inch overhang.

4 To prepare filling, combine apple slices, sugar, cinnamon, 1/4 teaspoon nutmeg and 1/4 teaspoon salt in large bowl; mix until well combined. Spoon into crust.

5 To prepare topping, stir together brown sugar, 3/4 cup flour and 1/2 teaspoon nutmeg in small bowl. Cut butter into brown sugar mixture until mixture crumbles. Sprinkle apples evenly over topping. Bake pie about 35 minutes or until topping is lightly browned and filling is bubbly. Cool on wire rack.

8 servings

APPLE CREAM PIE

LIZ BLAKE
BEAUMONT, TEXAS

3/4 cup sugar

2 tablespoons all-purpose flour

1 cup sour cream

1 egg, well beaten

1/2 teaspoon vanilla

1/8 teaspoon salt

2 cups finely chopped tart apples

1 (9-inch) unbaked pie shell

TOPPING

1/3 cup sugar

1 teaspoon cinnamon

1/3 cup all-purpose flour

1/4 cup butter, softened

1 Heat oven to 450°F.

2 In large bowl, combine 3/4 cup sugar and 2 tablespoons flour; add sour cream, egg, vanilla and salt. Beat at medium speed until smooth. Add apples; mix thoroughly. Pour into pie shell.

3 Bake 15 minutes. Reduce oven temperature to 325°F; bake an additional 30 minutes. In medium bowl, combine 1/3 cup sugar, cinnamon, 1/3 cup flour and butter; sprinkle over pie. Bake an additional 20 minutes or until crust is golden brown. Cool on wire rack. Store in refrigerator.

8 servings

RASPBERRY PIE

THERESA GAUDETTE
NORTH NEW PORTLAND, MAINE

2 (9-inch) baked pie shells

4 cups fresh raspberries

1 1/4 cups sugar

3 tablespoons cornstarch

1 tablespoon butter

1 Heat oven to 400°F.

2 Line 9-inch pie pan with one of the pie shells. In medium bowl, combine raspberries, sugar and cornstarch. Pour into crust; dot with butter. Top with remaining pie shell.

3 Bake 45 minutes or until crust is golden brown; cool on wire rack.

TIP *For a nice finish to top of pie, brush with beaten egg white and sprinkle with powdered sugar.

16 servings

FRENCH SILK PIE

MARGARET BENHAM
OKLAHOMA CITY, OKLAHOMA

1/2 cup butter, softened

1 1/2 cups powdered sugar

2 pasteurized eggs

2 (1-oz.) squares unsweetened chocolate, melted

1 teaspoon vanilla

1 (9-inch) baked pie shell

1 In medium bowl, beat butter and powdered sugar at high speed 5 minutes or until fluffy. Add eggs one at a time, beating 1 to 2 minutes after each addition. Add chocolate and vanilla to egg mixture; beat until light and fluffy.

2 Pour mixture into pie shell; refrigerate several hours or overnight. Serve topped with whipped cream and chocolate curls, if desired. Store in refrigerator.

8 servings

RASPBERRY PIE

CHAMPAGNE SWEET POTATO PIE

BRIGITTE LITTLE
EATONTOWN, NEW JERSEY

3 to 4 medium sweet potatoes, peeled, cubed

3 tablespoons butter

1/2 cup sugar

1/2 cup packed brown sugar

1/2 cup Champagne

1/2 cup orange juice

1/4 teaspoon nutmeg

1 teaspoon cinnamon

1/4 teaspoon ground ginger

2 teaspoons vanilla

2 eggs, separated

1/4 to 1/2 cup milk

1 (9-inch) graham-cracker pie shell

1 Heat oven to 350°F. Arrange sweet potatoes in 13x9-inch pan.

2 In medium saucepan, melt butter over low heat. Add sugars; stir until very thick. Add Champagne, orange juice, nutmeg, cinnamon, ginger and vanilla; blend well. Bring to a boil; simmer 2 minutes. Remove from heat; pour mixture over potatoes. Cover and bake 1 hour or until potatoes are very tender.

3 In large bowl, mash potatoes and cooking liquid until smooth. (Or cool potatoes slightly and puree in blender or food processor.) In separate bowl, beat egg whites at medium-high speed until soft peaks form. Beat egg yolks and milk into sweet potato mixture until creamy. Gently fold in egg whites.

4 Pour into pie shell; bake 30 minutes or until set. Garnish with chopped nuts and whipped cream, if desired. Store in refrigerator.

8 servings

FRESH STRAWBERRY GLAZED PIE

SHARON DECKER
CLYMER, PENNSYLVANIA

CRUST

1 1/2 cups graham-cracker crumbs

3 tablespoons sugar

1/3 cup melted butter

FILLING

6 cups small whole fresh strawberries (about 1 1/2 quarts)

1 cup sugar

3 tablespoons cornstarch

1/2 cup water

1 Heat oven to 350°F.

2 In large bowl, combine crumbs and 3 tablespoons sugar; add butter and mix thoroughly. Press mixture into 9-inch pie pan. Bake 10 minutes. Cool completely.

3 Mash 4 cups of the berries. In medium saucepan, stir together 1 cup sugar and cornstarch; gradually stir in water and mashed berries. Cook over medium heat, stirring constantly, until mixture thickens and boils. Boil and stir 1 minute. Cool completely.

4 Fill pie shell with remaining 2 cups berries. Pour glaze over berries; spread to edges of crust carefully to avoid pulling crumbs into glaze. Refrigerate at least 3 hours or until set. Store in refrigerator.

8 servings

JESSIE'S APPLE DUMPLINGS

PEGGY WINKWORTH
DURANGO, COLORADO

1 1/2 cups sugar

1 1/8 teaspoons cinnamon

5 tablespoons butter

1/8 teaspoon salt

1 *Sour Cream Pie Shell* (page 26), unbaked

4 apples, peeled, cored

2 cups water

1 Heat oven to 425°F.

2 In small bowl, combine 1/2 cup of the sugar, 1/8 teaspoon of the cinnamon, 1 tablespoon of the butter and salt; mix until well blended. Divide mixture among apples, placing in center of each apple.

3 Roll out dough on floured surface. Cut square of dough for each apple (dough should be large enough to wrap around apple). Wrap apples with dough. Place dumplings in 13x9-inch aluminum foil-lined pan.

4 In saucepan, combine water, remaining 1 cup sugar, remaining 1 teaspoon cinnamon and remaining 4 tablespoons butter. Simmer 10 minutes. Pour mixture over dumplings. Bake 40 to 45 minutes or until crust is golden and apples are tender. Serve warm or cool. Store in refrigerator.

6 servings

PEACH CRUMBLE

FANNIE KLINE
MILLERSBURG, OHIO

FILLING

5 cups peeled sliced fresh peaches

1 tablespoon lemon juice

1 cup sugar

2 tablespoons all-purpose flour

1/2 teaspoon nutmeg, freshly grated

TOPPING

2 1/2 cups all-purpose flour

1 cup butter

1/2 teaspoon salt

1/2 cup packed brown sugar

1/2 cup chopped pecans

1 Heat oven to 350°F. Spray 3-quart casserole with nonstick cooking spray.

2 Arrange peaches in bottom of pan; sprinkle with lemon juice. In medium bowl, stir together sugar, 2 tablespoons flour and nutmeg; mix with peaches. Set aside.

3 For topping, combine 2 1/2 cups flour, butter and salt with pastry blender until mixture crumbles. Stir in brown sugar and pecans. Sprinkle over peach mixture.

4 Bake 40 to 50 minutes or until juice bubbles. Cool slightly on wire rack; serve with vanilla ice cream, if desired. Store in refrigerator.

10 servings

GRANDMA BETTY'S UPSIDE-DOWN COBBLER

GRANDMA BETTY'S UPSIDE-DOWN COBBLER

CARLENE GOODEILL
CHICO, CALIFORNIA

¼ cup shortening

½ cup sugar

1 cup all-purpose flour

2 teaspoons baking powder

1 egg

½ cup milk

2 cups fresh berries or sliced fresh peaches

1 Heat oven to 350°F. Spray 8-inch round cake pan with nonstick cooking spray.

2 In medium bowl, combine shortening, sugar, flour, baking powder, egg and milk; mix until well blended. Pour batter into pan. Spoon berries over batter.

3 Bake 45 to 60 minutes or until toothpick inserted in center comes out clean. Cool on wire rack. Store in refrigerator.

6 servings

LEMON-BUTTERMILK PIE

SARAH ROARK
ROSSVILLE, ILLINOIS

4 eggs

¾ cup sugar

2 tablespoons all-purpose flour

1½ cups buttermilk

¼ cup melted butter

1 tablespoon grated lemon peel

3 tablespoons fresh lemon juice

1 teaspoon vanilla

1 (9-inch) unbaked pie shell

½ teaspoon cinnamon

1 Heat oven to 375°F.

2 In large bowl, beat eggs and sugar at medium speed until light and fluffy. Beat in flour, buttermilk, butter, lemon peel, lemon juice and vanilla. Pour into pie shell. Sprinkle with cinnamon.

3 Bake 20 to 30 minutes or until toothpick inserted in center comes out clean. Cool on wire rack. Store in refrigerator.

8 servings

BANANA-CARAMEL PIE

TAMMY RAYNES
NATCHITOCHES, LOUISIANA

¼ cup water

2 egg yolks, beaten

½ cup sugar

½ cup packed brown sugar

¼ cup all-purpose flour

¼ teaspoon salt

1 cup boiling water

1 tablespoon butter

½ teaspoon vanilla

3 to 4 medium bananas, sliced

1 (9-inch) baked pie shell

1 cup heavy cream, whipped

1 In medium saucepan, combine water and egg yolks. Add sugar, brown sugar, flour and salt; stir well. Gradually add boiling water, stirring constantly over medium-low heat 1 to 2 minutes or until mixture is thickened. Remove from heat; add butter and vanilla, stirring until butter melts. Cool 5 minutes, stirring occasionally.

2 Layer banana slices in pie shell; pour filling over bananas. Cover and refrigerate at least 2 hours. Spread whipped cream over pie. Store in refrigerator.

8 servings

YAM PRALINE PIE

LINNIE DAVIS
ELKHART, INDIANA

FILLING

2 eggs

1/2 cup sugar

1/2 cup packed brown sugar

1 teaspoon cinnamon

1/2 teaspoon nutmeg

1/2 teaspoon ground ginger

1/4 teaspoon salt

2 cups mashed cooked yams

3/4 cup milk

1 cup half-and-half

1 (9-inch) unbaked pie shell

TOPPING

1/3 cup chopped pecans

1/3 cup packed brown sugar

3 tablespoons butter

1 Heat oven to 400°F.

2 In large bowl, beat eggs at medium speed. Add sugar, 1/2 cup brown sugar, cinnamon, nutmeg, ginger and salt. Stir in yams. Gradually stir in milk and half-and-half. Pour mixture into pie shell.

3 Bake 10 minutes. Reduce oven temperature to 350°F; bake an additional 25 minutes.

4 To prepare topping, combine pecans, 1/3 cup brown sugar and butter in small bowl; mix until well combined. Sprinkle topping over pie. Bake 20 minutes or until toothpick inserted in center comes out clean. Cool completely on wire rack. Store in refrigerator.

8 servings

AUTUMN CARAMEL APPLE PIE

GWEN CAMPBELL
STERLING, VIRGINIA

4 cups Granny Smith apples, peeled, cored, thinly sliced

2 tablespoons apple juice or water

1 (9-inch) graham-cracker pie shell

3/4 cup packed brown sugar

3/4 cup graham-cracker crumbs

1 tablespoon all-purpose flour

1/2 teaspoon cinnamon

1/2 teaspoon nutmeg

1/4 teaspoon ground cardamom

1/4 cup unsalted melted butter

TOPPING

20 vanilla caramels, unwrapped

3 tablespoons milk

1/4 teaspoon rum extract

1 Heat oven to 350°F. In large saucepan, combine apple slices and apple juice; simmer 10 minutes. Pour mixture into large bowl to cool. Pour cooled mixture, including liquid, into pie shell.

2 In another large bowl, combine brown sugar, graham-cracker crumbs, flour, cinnamon, nutmeg, cardamom and butter; sprinkle evenly over apples. Bake 20 minutes or until apples are tender; remove from oven but do not turn oven off.

3 To prepare sauce, combine caramels and milk in medium saucepan over low heat. Stir until melted and smooth; stir in rum extract. Pour hot caramel sauce over pie; return pie to oven. Continue to bake an additional 10 minutes or until caramel just begins to bubble at edge of pie. Cool pie on wire rack.

8 servings

AUTUMN CARAMEL APPLE PIE

CREAM CHEESE PECAN PIE

CREAM CHEESE PECAN PIE

VIVIAN NIKANOW
CHICAGO, ILLINOIS

1 (8-oz.) pkg. cream cheese, softened

$1/3$ cup sugar

4 eggs

2 teaspoons vanilla

1 (9-inch) unbaked pie shell

$1 1/4$ cups coarsely chopped pecans

1 cup light corn syrup

$1/4$ teaspoon salt

1 Heat oven to 375°F.

2 In large bowl, beat together cream cheese, sugar, 1 of the eggs and 1 teaspoon of the vanilla at high speed until smooth. Pour mixture into pie shell. Sprinkle pecans over cheese mixture.

3 In small bowl, combine remaining 3 eggs, corn syrup, salt and remaining 1 teaspoon of the vanilla; pour mixture over pecans.

4 Bake 40 minutes or until set. Cool on wire rack. Store in refrigerator.

8 servings

CHOCOLATE MOUSSE PIE

CHRISTINA POOL
SALEM, OREGON

CRUST

$1 2/3$ cups all-purpose flour

$1/2$ teaspoon salt

$1/2$ cup shortening

3 to 4 tablespoons cold water

FILLING

$1 1/2$ cups miniature marshmallows or 16 large marshmallows

$1/2$ cup milk

1 (8-oz.) bar milk chocolate

1 cup heavy cream

1 Heat oven to 475°F.

2 To prepare crust, combine flour and salt in medium bowl. With pastry blender or two knives, work shortening into flour mixture until mixture crumbles. Sprinkle with water, 1 tablespoon at a time, tossing with fork until flour is moistened and pastry almost cleans side of bowl. Gather pastry into ball; shape into disk on lightly floured cloth-covered surface. Roll pastry to $1/8$ inch thickness with floured cloth-covered rolling pin. Line 9-inch pie pan with dough; press firmly against bottom and sides. Prick bottom and sides thoroughly with fork. Bake 8 to 10 minutes or until light brown; cool.

3 To prepare filling, heat marshmallows, milk and chocolate in medium saucepan over low heat, stirring constantly until melted and mixture is smooth. Refrigerate, stirring occasionally, until mixture mounds slightly when dropped from spoon. Beat cream in chilled bowl at high speed. Fold chocolate mixture into whipped cream. Pour into pie shell. Refrigerate about 8 hours or until set. Spread with whipped cream and garnish with chocolate curls, if desired. Store in refrigerator.

8 servings

COOKIES

SOUR CREAM CUT-OUT COOKIES (page 65)

BANANA OATMEAL ROCKS

LINDA ZIERDEN
ST. CLOUD, MINNESOTA

1 1/2 cups all-purpose flour

1/2 teaspoon baking soda

1 teaspoon salt

1/4 teaspoon nutmeg

3/4 teaspoon cinnamon

3/4 cup shortening

1 cup sugar

1 egg

1 cup mashed bananas

1 3/4 cup old-fashioned or quick-cooking oats

1/2 cup walnuts

1 Heat oven to 325°F. Line several baking sheets with parchment paper.

2 In large bowl, mix together flour, baking soda, salt, nutmeg and cinnamon.

3 In another large bowl, beat shortening at medium speed until fluffy. Add sugar, egg, bananas, oats and walnuts; beat until blended. Add flour mixture; mix until blended. Drop by teaspoonfuls about 2 inches apart on baking sheets. Bake about 20 minutes or until brown. Cool on wire rack.

About 4 dozen

INSIDE-OUT CHOCOLATE CHIP COOKIES

CHRISTINA POOL
SALEM, OREGON

1 cup sugar

3/4 cup packed brown sugar

3/4 cup butter, softened

1/2 cup shortening

2 eggs

1 teaspoon vanilla

2 1/2 cups all-purpose flour

1/2 cup unsweetened cocoa

1 teaspoon baking soda

1/4 teaspoon salt

1 1/2 cups white chocolate chips (9 oz.)

1 cup chopped nuts, if desired

1 Heat oven to 350°F. Line several baking sheets with parchment paper.

2 In large bowl, beat sugar, brown sugar, butter, shortening, eggs and vanilla at medium speed until well blended. Add flour, cocoa, baking soda, salt, chips and nuts; beat until well blended.

3 Drop dough by rounded teaspoonfuls about 2 inches apart onto baking sheets. Bake 10 to 12 minutes or until set. Cool 2 minutes on baking sheets; cool completely on wire racks.

4 dozen

INSIDE-OUT CHOCOLATE CHIP COOKIES

WALNUT BUTTER COOKIES (SANDWICHED WITH JELLY)

WALNUT BUTTER COOKIES (SANDWICHED WITH JELLY)

JEFFREY A. BUSSE
SHRUB OAK, NEW YORK

1 cup butter, softened

1 cup sugar

3 eggs, separated

1 teaspoon vanilla

$1/8$ teaspoon salt

3 cups all-purpose flour

$1/2$ teaspoon baking powder

$1/2$ lb. walnuts, finely chopped

$1/4$ cup decorative sugar (red or green)

Assorted fruit jellies

1 In large bowl, beat butter at medium speed until fluffy. Beat in sugar, egg yolks, vanilla and salt. Stir in flour and baking powder until well blended. Refrigerate 1 hour.

2 Heat oven to 350°F. Line several baking sheets with parchment paper.

3 Roll out dough to $1/8$=inch thickness; cut out one-half of dough with $2^1/2$-inch round cutters. Cut out remaining dough with a $2^1/2$-inch doughnut cutter. Combine walnuts and decorative sugar. Brush doughnut-shaped cut-outs with egg white; sprinkle with walnut-sugar mixture. Arrange about 2 inches apart on baking sheets. Bake 6 to 7 minutes or until light brown; cool on wire rack.

4 Spread bottom side of round cookies with desired flavor jellies; top with doughnut-shaped cookies, decorated tops up.

About 3 dozen

PEANUTTY FUDGE PUDDLES

TERI HARVEY
CORVALLIS, OREGON

$1^1/4$ cups all-purpose flour

$3/4$ teaspoon baking soda

$1/2$ teaspoon salt

$1/2$ cup sugar

$1/2$ cup packed brown sugar

$1/2$ cup butter, softened

$1/2$ cup peanut butter

1 egg

$1/2$ teaspoon vanilla

FUDGE FILLING

1 cup semisweet chocolate chips (6 oz.)

$2/3$ cup sweetened condensed milk

$1/2$ teaspoon vanilla

$1/4$ cup dry-roasted peanuts

1 Heat oven to 325°F. Spray miniature ($1^3/4$-inch) muffin cups with nonstick cooking spray.

2 In large bowl, combine flour, baking soda and salt; set aside. In another large bowl, beat sugar, brown sugar, butter and peanut butter at medium speed until blended and fluffy. Add egg and $1/2$ teaspoon vanilla. Beat flour mixture into butter mixture. Stir well. Refrigerate 1 hour.

3 Shape dough into 1-inch balls. Place in muffin cups. Bake 14 to 16 minutes or until lightly browned. Remove from oven and immediately press "wells" into center of each cookie with melon baller. Cool in pan 5 minutes. Cool completely on wire rack.

4 In microwave-safe bowl, melt chips in microwave. Stir milk and $1/2$ teaspoon vanilla into melted chips until smooth. Place a few peanuts into each cookie's "well" and fill with fudge filling. Allow to cool on counter until firm. Store in airtight container.

4 dozen

INDULGENT BARS

& BROWNIES

KEY LIME BARS (page 80)

GOOEY PEANUT BUTTER BARS

GOOEY PEANUT BUTTER BARS

KIMBERLY HAYES
OKLAHOMA CITY, OKLAHOMA

2 cups butter

1 cup sugar

1 cup packed brown sugar

2 eggs

2 cups peanut butter

2 teaspoons vanilla

2 cups all-purpose flour

$\frac{1}{2}$ teaspoon baking powder

$\frac{1}{2}$ cup chopped pecans or walnuts

$\frac{1}{2}$ cup semisweet chocolate chips (3 oz.)

$\frac{1}{2}$ cup white chocolate chips (3 oz.)

$\frac{1}{2}$ cup butterscotch chips (3 oz.)

1 Heat oven to 350°F. Line 13x9-inch pan with aluminum foil.

2 In large bowl, combine butter, sugar and brown sugar until well blended. Add eggs and blend again. Add peanut butter and vanilla, blending well.

3 In another bowl, combine flour and baking powder. Stir into peanut butter mixture. Spread batter evenly into pan. Sprinkle nuts and chips evenly over top. Bake 30 to 35 minutes or until center is firm. Cool completely on wire rack. Cut into 2x1-inch bars.

4 dozen bars

SENSATIONAL MINT BROWNIES

CHERYL PETERSON

$1\frac{1}{2}$ cups melted butter

3 cups sugar

1 tablespoon vanilla

5 eggs

2 cups all-purpose flour

1 cup unsweetened cocoa

1 teaspoon baking powder

1 teaspoon salt

24 ($1\frac{1}{2}$-inch) chocolate-covered peppermint patties

1 Heat oven to 350°F. Spray 13x9-inch pan with nonstick cooking spray.

2 In large bowl, whisk together butter, sugar and vanilla. Add eggs; stir until well blended. Stir in flour, cocoa, baking powder and salt; blend well. Spread remaining batter in pan, reserving 2 cups batter. Arrange peppermint patties in single layer over batter about $\frac{1}{2}$ inch apart. Spread reserved 2 cups batter over patties.

3 Bake 50 to 55 minutes or until brownies begin to pull away from sides of pan. Cool completely in pan. Cut into squares.

3 dozen brownies

CREAM CHEESE BROWNIES

KAREN COLEMAN
FORT FAIRFIELD, MAINE

1 (8-oz.) pkg. cream cheese

1⅓ cups sugar

3 eggs

¼ teaspoon almond extract

2 (1-oz.) squares semisweet chocolate

½ cup butter

¾ cup all-purpose flour

½ teaspoon salt

½ teaspoon baking powder

½ cup chopped nuts

1 Heat oven to 350°F. Spray 8-inch square pan with nonstick cooking spray.

2 In large bowl, beat cream cheese, ⅓ cup of the sugar, 1 of the eggs and almond extract; set aside. In small saucepan, heat chocolate and butter over medium-high heat until melted; set aside.

3 In another large bowl, beat remaining 2 eggs and remaining 1 cup sugar with chocolate mixture. In small bowl, combine flour, salt and baking powder; stir into chocolate mixture and mix well.

4 Pour one-half of chocolate mixture into pan. Spread cream cheese mixture over top. Pour remaining batter over cream cheese and sprinkle with nuts. Bake 40 minutes or until set. Cool in pan. Cut into bars.

2 dozen brownies

KEY LIME BARS

CHARLOTTE WARD
HILTON HEAD, SOUTH CAROLINA

BARS

2 cups all-purpose flour

1 cup butter, softened

½ cup powdered sugar

FILLING

2 cups sugar

¼ cup all-purpose flour

1 teaspoon baking powder

4 eggs

½ cup fresh or bottled Key lime juice

¼ cup grated Key or regular lime peel

Powdered sugar

1 Heat oven to 350°F.

2 In medium bowl, combine 2 cups flour, butter and ½ cup powdered sugar; mix thoroughly. Press mixture into 13x9-inch pan. Bake 10 minutes. Set aside.

3 In large bowl, combine 2 cups sugar, ¼ cup flour, baking powder and eggs; mix until well blended. Gently stir in lime juice and peel. Carefully pour over hot crust. Bake an additional 25 to 30 minutes or until edges are light brown and filling is set. Cool completely on wire rack; sprinkle with powdered sugar. Cut into 1½-inch squares. Store in refrigerator.

About 4 dozen bars

KEY LIME BARS

CREME DE MENTHE BROWNIES WITH A CRUST

CREME DE MENTHE BROWNIES WITH A CRUST

SUSAN BETTINGER
BATTLE CREEK, MICHIGAN

BROWNIES

1 cup sugar

$\frac{1}{2}$ cup butter

4 eggs

2 cups chocolate syrup

1 teaspoon vanilla

1 cup all-purpose flour

$\frac{1}{2}$ teaspoon salt

FROSTING

2 cups powdered sugar

3 tablespoons crème de menthe syrup*

$\frac{1}{2}$ cup butter

TOPPING

1 cup semisweet chocolate chips (6 oz.)

$1\frac{1}{3}$ cups butter

1 Heat oven to 350°F. Spray 13x9-inch pan with nonstick cooking spray.

2 In large bowl, beat 1 cup sugar and $\frac{1}{2}$ cup butter. Beat in eggs, chocolate syrup and vanilla. Stir in flour and salt; mix until well blended. Pour into pan. Bake 30 minutes or just until brownies start to pull away from sides of pan. Cool on wire rack.

3 In large bowl, combine 2 cups sugar, crème de menthe syrup and $\frac{1}{2}$ cup butter; mix until smooth. Spread frosting over cooled brownies.

4 In small saucepan, heat chocolate chips and $1\frac{1}{3}$ cups butter over medium-high heat until melted. Remove from heat; cool. Pour chocolate topping over frosting. Let stand until chocolate is set. Cut into 2-inch squares or triangles.

TIP *Crème de menthe syrup can be found in the ice cream section of most grocery stores.

About 3 dozen brownies

BROWNIE ICE CREAM CONES

MARY STRONG
PLEASANTON, TEXAS

1 (4-oz.) bar German sweet chocolate

$\frac{1}{4}$ cup butter

$\frac{3}{4}$ cup sugar

2 eggs

$\frac{1}{2}$ cup all-purpose flour

$\frac{1}{2}$ cup chopped walnuts

1 teaspoon vanilla

24 flat-bottomed ice cream cones

24 scoops ice cream

Chocolate sprinkles

1 In large microwave-safe bowl, microwave chocolate and butter on High, stirring occasionally, until melted. Remove from microwave; cool. Add sugar and eggs; mix well. Stir in flour, walnuts and vanilla.

2 Heat oven to 350°F. Meanwhile, place cones in muffin cups. Fill each cone half full of chocolate mixture. Bake 20 to 22 minutes or until toothpick inserted in center comes out almost clean. Top each cone with scoop of ice cream; top with sprinkles.

2 dozen cones

MOUSSES & MERINGUES

RICE PUDDING WITH RASPBERRY SAUCE (page 94)

ESPRESSO BREAD PUDDING WITH
ALMOND-FLAVORED LIQUEUR CUSTARD SAUCE

ESPRESSO BREAD PUDDING WITH ALMOND-FLAVORED LIQUEUR CUSTARD SAUCE

CHRISTOPHER FOGERTY
GREENTOWN, INDIANA

BREAD PUDDING

6 eggs, separated

1¼ cups sugar

1 tablespoon vanilla

2 cups heavy cream

¼ cup unsalted butter

2 tablespoons coarsely ground espresso beans

1 cup semisweet chocolate chips (6 oz.)

1 lb. bakery-style* cinnamon doughnuts, broken into 1-inch pieces

SAUCE

10 egg yolks

1 cup sugar

3 cups whole milk

3 tablespoons almond-flavored liqueur

2 teaspoons vanilla

1 Heat oven to 325°F. Spray 12 (6-oz.) custard cups with nonstick cooking spray; set aside.

2 Separate eggs into 2 medium bowls. Into egg yolks, whisk ¾ cup of the sugar and 1 tablespoon vanilla; set aside.

3 In medium saucepan, combine cream, butter and espresso powder. Bring mixture to a simmer over medium-high heat, stirring frequently. Strain mixture through fine mesh strainer and return to pan over medium heat until hot. Gradually pour espresso mixture into yolk mixture, whisking constantly. Stir in chocolate chips until melted and smooth.

4 Beat egg whites at medium speed until soft peaks form; slowly add remaining ½ cup sugar; beat until stiff but not dry. Fold into chocolate mixture. Add doughnuts; toss to coat evenly. Fill custard cups with pudding mixture; let stand 1 hour.

5 Place custard cups in large roasting pan with 1 to 2 inches water in bottom. Bake 50 to 60 minutes or until toothpick inserted in center comes out clean. Invert puddings onto individual plates.

6 To prepare sauce, whisk egg yolks and 1 cup sugar in large bowl until well blended. In medium saucepan, bring milk to a simmer over medium heat. Whisk hot milk slowly into egg mixture. Return to saucepan over low heat, stirring constantly. Cook 8 to 12 minutes or until mixture just coats back of metal spoon. Strain custard through fine mesh strainer into medium bowl; whisk in liqueur and 2 teaspoons vanilla. Cool to room temperature; refrigerate 3 hours. Serve with bread pudding. Store in refrigerator.

TIP *Use yeast-raised doughnuts.

12 servings

DOUBLE CHOCOLATE FUDGE CAKE

DOUBLE CHOCOLATE FUDGE CAKE

AMY SMOUSE
CORTEZ, COLORADO

CAKE

2 1/4 cups semisweet chocolate chips (14 oz.)

2 cups butter

1 1/2 cups sugar

1 cup half-and-half

1 tablespoon vanilla

1/2 teaspoon salt

8 eggs

GLAZE

2 tablespoons butter

1 cup semisweet chocolate (6 oz.)

3 tablespoons milk

2 tablespoons white corn syrup

1 cup heavy cream

GARNISH

1 cup heavy cream

1 cup assorted raspberries, blackberries

1 Heat oven to 350°F. Spray 9-inch round cake pan with nonstick cooking spray.

2 Combine 2 1/4 cups chocolate chips, 2 cups butter, sugar, half-and-half, vanilla and salt in medium saucepan over medium-low heat. Cook, stirring frequently, 2 minutes or until chocolate is melted. Remove from heat. In large bowl, beat eggs until well blended; stir chocolate mixture into eggs. Pour into prepared pan.

3 Bake 45 minutes; cool completely on wire rack. Wrap in plastic wrap; refrigerate 6 hours.

4 Remove cake from pan. To prepare glaze, melt 2 tablespoons butter and 1 cup chocolate chips in medium saucepan over low heat; remove from heat. Beat in milk and corn syrup. Spread warm glaze over top and sides of cake. In medium bowl, beat cream at high speed until soft peaks form. Garnish cake with whipped cream and berries.

24 servings

GRAHAM-CRACKER CAKE

MARY J. EDGAR
CINCINNATI, OHIO

CAKE

1/2 cup butter

1 cup sugar

3 eggs, separated

1 teaspoon vanilla

3 cups crushed graham crackers

6 tablespoons all-purpose flour

1 1/2 teaspoons baking powder

1/8 teaspoon nutmeg

3/4 cup milk

1/4 teaspoon cinnamon

1/2 cup chopped walnuts

ICING

1/2 cup butter

1 (8-oz.) pkg. cream cheese

1 (16-oz.) pkg. powdered sugar

2 teaspoons vanilla

8 walnut halves

1 Heat oven to 350°F. Spray 2 (8-inch) round cake pans with nonstick cooking spray.

2 In large bowl, beat 1/2 cup butter and sugar at high speed until fluffy. Beat in egg yolks and 1 teaspoon vanilla. Combine graham cracker crumbs, flour, baking powder, cinnamon and nutmeg; add alternately with milk to butter mixture.

3 In another large bowl, beat egg whites at high speed until stiff peaks form. Fold egg whites into batter. Pour into pans.

4 Bake 25 to 30 minutes or until toothpick inserted in center comes out clean. Cool in pans 5 minutes; remove from pans and cool on wire rack.

5 To prepare frosting, beat 1/2 cup butter and cream cheese at high speed in medium bowl until fluffy. Add powdered sugar and 2 teaspoons vanilla; beat until light and fluffy. Spread frosting over cakes. Garnish with walnuts. Store in refrigerator.

8 servings

JO'S PECAN RUM CAKE

PEGGY WINKWORTH
DURANGO, COLORADO

CAKE

¾ cup finely chopped pecans

1 (18.5-oz.) box butter-recipe yellow cake mix

1 (3.4-oz.) pkg. instant vanilla pudding mix

4 eggs

½ cup light rum

½ cup vegetable oil

½ cup water

½ cup butter

GLAZE

½ cup butter

½ cup rum

1 cup sugar

¼ cup water

1 Heat oven to 325°F. Spray 12-cup Bundt pan with nonstick cooking spray.

2 Sprinkle pecans in bottom of pan. In large bowl, combine cake mix, pudding mix, eggs, ½ cup rum, oil, ½ cup water and ½ cup butter; beat at medium speed about 3 minutes or until smooth. Pour into pan.

3 Bake 50 to 60 minutes or until toothpick inserted in center comes out clean. Cool 20 minutes in pans. With thin spatula, loosen edges and center of cake. Invert cake onto serving plate. Poke holes in cake with long-tined fork or bamboo skewer.

4 To prepare glaze, in small saucepan, boil butter, ½ cup rum, 1 cup sugar and ¼ cup water 3 minutes. Drizzle glaze over cake. Cover cake with aluminum foil and refrigerate up to 3 days.

16 servings

LEMON-CREAM CHEESE POUND CAKE

PEGGY YAMAGUCHI-LAZAR
EUGENE, OREGON

CAKE

3 cups sugar

1¼ cups butter, softened

1 (8-oz.) pkg. cream cheese, softened

3 tablespoons lemon juice

2 teaspoons vanilla

1 teaspoon lemon extract

½ teaspoon orange extract

⅛ teaspoon salt

6 eggs

2¾ cups all-purpose flour

GLAZE

1 cup powdered sugar

1 tablespoon butter

2 teaspoons grated lemon peel

2 tablespoons lemon juice

1 Heat oven to 325°F. Spray 10-inch tube pan or 12-cup Bundt pan with nonstick cooking spray; lightly flour.

2 In large bowl, beat sugar, 1¼ cups butter and cream cheese at high speed until fluffy. Beat in lemon juice, vanilla, lemon extract, orange extract and salt. Add eggs one at a time, beating after each addition. Add flour; beat until smooth. Spread in pan.

3 Bake 1 hour or until golden brown and toothpick inserted in center comes out clean. Cool 10 minutes; remove from pan. Cool completely on wire rack.

4 To prepare glaze, mix powdered sugar, 1 tablespoon butter, lemon peel and 2 tablespoons lemon juice in another large bowl. Add additional lemon juice, 1 teaspoon at a time, until smooth. Spread glaze over cake, allowing some to drizzle down side.

16 servings

LEMON-CREAM CHEESE POUND CAKE

APPLE CAKE

APPLE CAKE

RITA HASHEMI
DUBLIN, OHIO

$^3/_4$ cup butter

$1^3/_4$ cups sugar

$^1/_2$ cup water

$^3/_4$ teaspoon cinnamon

2 Granny Smith apples, peeled, thinly sliced

3 egg yolks

2 eggs

2 tablespoons brandy

2 teaspoons vanilla

1 cup all-purpose flour

1 teaspoon baking powder

1 Heat oven to 350°F. Spray 9-inch round cake pan with nonstick cooking spray; lightly dust with sugar, tapping out excess.

2 In large saucepan, combine $^1/_4$ cup of the butter, $^3/_4$ cup of the sugar, water and cinnamon; bring to a boil. Reduce heat and simmer 5 minutes. Arrange apples decoratively in bottom of pan; top with syrup.

3 In large bowl, beat together remaining $^1/_2$ cup butter and 1 cup sugar until smooth. Beat in egg yolks, eggs, brandy and vanilla until well blended. Fold in flour and baking powder. Spoon batter over apples.

4 Bake 35 to 40 minutes. Remove from oven; cool 3 minutes. Loosen edges of cake; invert onto serving platter. Serve warm.

8 servings

I'LL-START-MY-DIET-NEXT-WEEK CUPCAKES

DIANNA HOWARD
COOS BAY, OREGON

CAKE

3 cups all-purpose flour

2 cups sugar

$^1/_2$ cup unsweetened cocoa

2 teaspoons baking soda

1 teaspoon salt

$^2/_3$ cup vegetable oil

2 cups water

2 tablespoons vinegar

2 teaspoons vanilla

FILLING

1 (8-oz.) pkg. cream cheese, softened

1 egg

$^1/_3$ cup sugar

$^1/_4$ teaspoon salt

1 cup semisweet chocolate chips (6 oz.)

1 Heat oven to 350°F. Line 24 muffin cups with paper liners.

2 In large bowl, combine flour, 2 cups sugar, cocoa, baking soda and 1 teaspoon salt; set aside. In another large bowl, combine oil, water, vinegar and vanilla. Slowly combine flour mixture and oil mixture until smooth. Fill muffin cups two-thirds full.

3 To prepare filling, beat cream cheese, egg, $^1/_3$ cup sugar and $^1/_4$ teaspoon salt in another large bowl at medium speed until fluffy. Stir in chocolate chips. Drop heaping teaspoonful onto each cupcake.

4 Bake 25 minutes. Remove from pan; cool on wire rack. Store in refrigerator.

2 dozen cupcakes

THE ULTIMATE FLOURLESS CHOCOLATE CAKE

BRENDA JONES
LEXINGTON, SOUTH CAROLINA

1 (1-lb.) block semisweet chocolate

1/2 lb. unsalted butter, cut into chunks

1/4 cup strong coffee

8 large eggs, cold

1 Adjust oven rack to lower middle position; heat oven to 325°F. Line bottom of 8-inch springform pan with parchment paper; spray sides of pan with nonstick cooking spray. Wrap outside of pan with heavy-duty aluminum foil; place in large roasting pan.

2 Melt chocolate, butter and coffee in large heat-proof bowl over pan of barely simmering water until smooth and very warm, stirring occasionally. Or, heat in microwave-safe bowl at medium power 4 to 6 minutes, stirring occasionally. Meanwhile, in large bowl, beat eggs at high speed 5 minutes.

3 Fold in one-third of eggs into chocolate mixture using large rubber spatula only until mixed; fold in remaining egg mixture until mixture is homogenous.

4 Pour batter into pan; smooth surface with spatula. Set roasting pan on oven rack and pour enough boiling water to come about halfway up side of springform pan.

5 Bake 22 to 25 minutes or until cake has risen slightly, edges are just beginning to set and thin crust has formed on surface.

6 Remove cake from water bath; set on wire rack. Cool to room temperature. Cover and refrigerate overnight. About 30 minutes before serving, remove pan sides, invert cake onto sheet of parchment paper. Peel off paper; turn right-side-up on serving plate.

8 servings

CHERRY BLUSH CAKE WITH SABAYON

PAM MILLER
FALCON, COLORADO

CAKE

1/2 cup butter, softened

1/2 cup whipped cream cheese

3 cups sugar

6 eggs

4 1/2 cups all-purpose flour

1 teaspoon baking powder

2 teaspoons cherry extract

1/2 cup maraschino cherry juice

30 maraschino cherries, chopped, patted dry with paper towel

SABAYON SAUCE

8 egg yolks

2/3 cup sugar

1 cup dry sherry

1 cup heavy cream

Cherry brandy, if desired

Dark chocolate sauce

Chocolate-dipped cherries, if desired

1 Heat oven to 325°F. Spray 10-inch tube pan with nonstick cooking spray.

2 In large bowl, beat butter and cream cheese at high speed until blended. Slowly add 3 cups sugar; beat until light and fluffy. Add eggs one at a time, beating well after each addition. Combine 4 cups of the flour with baking powder; add to butter mixture and blend well. Stir in cherry extract and juice. Toss diced cherries in remaining 1/2 cup flour. Stir cherries and flour into batter; mix well. Pour batter into pan.

3 Bake 1 1/4 to 1 1/2 hours or until toothpick inserted in center comes out clean. Cool in pan 15 minutes. Remove from pan; invert cake onto wire rack. Cool completely.

4 To prepare sabayon sauce, fill large saucepan half full of water; simmer. In medium bowl, beat egg yolks and 2/3 cup sugar at medium speed 2 minutes. Mix in sherry. Place bowl over simmering water. (Do not allow bottom of bowl to touch water.) Beat until mixture doubles in volume and reaches 160°F on candy thermometer.

5 Pour into clean bowl; refrigerate about 1 hour or until cool. Beat cream until stiff peaks form; fold into sauce.

6 Arrange slices of cake on plate. Drizzle with cherry brandy. Drizzle with dark chocolate sauce. Garnish with chocolate-dipped cherries. Store in refrigerator.

16 servings

CHERRY BLUSH CAKE WITH SABAYON

CHERRY NUT CHIFFON CAKE

LINDA ALBERTS
SUN PRAIRIE, WISCONSIN

CAKE

2 cups all-purpose flour

1 1/2 cups sugar

1 tablespoon baking powder

1 teaspoon salt

1/2 cup vegetable oil

7 eggs, separated

1/2 cup water

1/4 cup maraschino cherry juice

1 teaspoon vanilla

1/2 teaspoon cream of tartar

1/2 cup finely chopped maraschino cherries, well drained

1/2 cup chopped nuts

ICING

3 1/2 cups powdered sugar

1/2 cup shortening

1/2 teaspoon salt

3 tablespoons maraschino cherry juice

3 tablespoons water

1 teaspoon lemon juice

1 Heat oven to 325°F.

2 In large bowl, combine flour, sugar, baking powder and 1 teaspoon salt. Make a well; add oil, egg yolks, 1/2 cup water, 1/4 cup cherry juice and vanilla. Beat at medium speed 1 minute or until smooth. In another large bowl, add cream of tartar to egg whites. Beat at medium speed until egg whites form stiff peaks. Pour egg yolk mixture gradually over beaten egg whites; gently fold with rubber spatula. Do not stir. Fold in cherries and nuts. Pour immediately into ungreased 10-inch tube pan.

3 Bake 55 minutes. Increase temperature to 350°F; bake an additional 10 to 15 minutes or until cake springs back when touched. Turn pan upside down over heatproof funnel until completely cooled. Loosen with spatula.

4 To prepare icing, beat powdered sugar with shortening and 1/2 teaspoon salt in large bowl at medium speed until blended. Stir in 3 tablespoons cherry juice, 3 tablespoons water and lemon juice; beat at medium speed until smooth. Cover tops and sides with icing.

8 servings

COFFEE-FLAVORED CAKE

ESTHER BUSEY
OKLAHOMA CITY, OKLAHOMA

1 (18.5-oz.) box devil's food cake mix

4 eggs

1 cup sour cream

1 cup coffee-flavored liqueur

1/2 cup melted butter

1 cup semisweet chocolate chips (6 oz.)

1 Heat oven to 350°F. Spray 12-cup Bundt pan with nonstick cooking spray; lightly flour.

2 In large bowl, combine cake mix, eggs, sour cream, liqueur and butter; beat at medium speed 3 to 5 minutes or until thoroughly blended. Stir in chocolate chips. Pour in pan.

3 Bake 50 to 60 minutes or until toothpick inserted near center comes out clean. Cool in pan 30 minutes. Remove from pan; invert onto wire rack. Cool completely.

16 servings

DATE PUDDING CAKE

LYNDA BURTON
HOUSTON, TEXAS

1 1/2 cups packed brown sugar

1 1/2 cups water

1 cup sugar

1 cup all-purpose flour

1 teaspoon baking powder

1/8 teaspoon salt

1/8 teaspoon salt

1 cup milk

1 teaspoon vanilla

1 cup chopped dates

1 cup chopped walnuts

1 Heat oven to 325°F. Combine brown sugar and water in medium saucepan; bring to a boil over high heat. Boil 5 minutes. Pour mixture into 3-quart casserole; cool.

2 In large bowl, combine sugar, flour, baking powder, salt, milk, vanilla, dates and walnuts; mix well. Pour over brown sugar layer.

3 Bake 35 to 40 minutes, increasing heat to 350°F during last 15 minutes of baking. Remove from oven; cool 5 minutes. Loosen cake with sharp knife. Invert cake onto serving platter.

16 servings

FRESH BERRY CAKE

DANIELA RAGUSA BALL
SALEM, OREGON

1 cup fresh strawberries

1 cup fresh blueberries

1 cup fresh raspberries

2 teaspoons grated lemon peel

1/2 cup sugar

1/2 cup orange-flavored liqueur or orange juice

1 (9 oz.) prepared angel food cake

1 In medium saucepan, cook berries, lemon peel, sugar and liqueur over medium-low heat until mixture begins to break down and bubble. Do not let mixture overcook; berries should remain whole. Set aside.

2 Cut cake into 2-inch pieces. Line cake pieces along bottom and sides of 3-quart casserole. Pour berry mixture into center of bowl; cover berry mixture completely with additional cake pieces.

3 Cover a heavy can with aluminum foil; place over top of cake. Refrigerate cake overnight. To serve, remove can and invert cake onto serving platter; decorate with additional berries, if desired. Store in refrigerator.

6 servings

PUMPKIN ROLL

PAM MILLIGAN
ARROYO GRANDE, CALIFORNIA

CAKE

3 eggs

1 cup sugar

2/3 cup pumpkin

1 teaspoon lemon juice

3/4 cup all-purpose flour

1 teaspoon baking powder

1/2 teaspoon salt

2 teaspoons cinnamon

1 teaspoon ground ginger

1/2 teaspoon nutmeg

1 cup chopped pecans

FILLING

1 cup powdered sugar

1/4 cup softened butter

1 (8-oz.) pkg. cream cheese, softened

1/2 teaspoon vanilla

2 tablespoons sweetened condensed milk

1 Heat oven to 350°F. Spray 15$^{1/2}$x10$^{1/2}$x1-inch baking pan with nonstick cooking spray. Line bottom of pan with parchment paper.

2 In medium bowl, beat eggs at high speed 5 minutes. Gradually add sugar, pumpkin and lemon juice. In separate bowl, mix flour, baking powder, salt, cinnamon, ginger and nutmeg; add to pumpkin mixture. Pour into pan. Sprinkle with pecans.

3 Bake 15 minutes or until toothpick inserted in center comes out clean.

4 Generously sift powdered sugar onto clean dish towel; invert cake onto towel. Carefully peel off parchment paper and lightly sift powdered sugar over cake. Roll up cake with towel from narrow end; let cool at least 30 minutes.

5 To prepare filling, beat powdered sugar, butter, cream cheese, vanilla and condensed milk in large bowl at medium speed until smooth. Unroll cake; spread with filling. Roll up again. Dust with powdered sugar. To serve, cut into 1-inch-thick slices. Store in refrigerator.

10 servings

OCCASION DESSERTS

CLAUDIA'S PUMPKIN-TOFFEE
CHEESECAKE (page 136)

APPLE AUTUMN CHEESECAKE

CLAUDIA WENDEL
FRESNO, CALIFORNIA

1 cup graham-cracker crumbs

3 tablespoons plus about 1 cup sugar

1 teaspoon cinnamon

1/4 cup butter

3/4 cup finely chopped pecans, if desired

2 (8-oz.) pkg. cream cheese, softened

2 eggs

1/2 teaspoon vanilla

4 cups peeled sliced apples

1/4 cup superfine sugar*

1 Heat oven to 350°F. Spray 9-inch springform pan with nonstick cooking spray.

2 In medium bowl, combine crumbs, 3 tablespoons of the sugar, 1/2 teaspoon of the cinnamon, butter and 1/2 cup of the pecans thoroughly; press mixture into pan. Refrigerate crust until filling is prepared.

3 In large bowl, blend cream cheese with 1/2 cup sugar. Add eggs one at a time, mixing well after each addition; add vanilla. Pour mixture into pan. Toss together apples, remaining 1/2 cup sugar, remaining 1/2 teaspoon cinnamon and remaining 1/4 cup pecans. Arrange apple slices on top of cheesecake batter; sprinkle with superfine sugar.

4 Bake 1 hour and 10 minutes or until nearly set. Cool on wire rack. Drizzle with caramel syrup before serving, if desired. Store in refrigerator.

TIP *Superfine sugar can be found with beverage ingredients in the grocery store, or process regular granulated sugar in blender until very finely ground.

12 servings

MINI CHEESECAKES

SUSAN DROBNY
ARLINGTON HEIGHTS, ILLINOIS

12 vanilla wafers

2 (8-oz.) pkg. cream cheese

1 teaspoon vanilla

1/2 cup sugar

2 eggs

1 Heat oven to 325°F. Line 12 (2 1/2 x 1 1/4-inch) muffin cups with foil liners. Place 1 wafer, flat side down, in each cup. Beat cream cheese, vanilla and sugar at medium speed until well blended. Add eggs; mix well. Pour over wafers, filling three-fourths full.

2 Bake 25 minutes. Cool in pan on wire rack; remove from pan when cool and refrigerate. Top with fruit, preserves, nuts or chocolate, if desired. Store in refrigerator.

12 mini cheesecakes

ITALIAN RICOTTA CHEESECAKE

LORRAINE MAGUR
WASHINGTONVILLE, NEW YORK

1/4 cup corn flake crumbs

2 lbs. whole milk ricotta

1 1/2 cups sugar

4 tablespoons all-purpose flour

2 teaspoons vanilla

1 cup sour cream

1 cup heavy cream, whipped

6 eggs

1 Heat oven to 400°F. Spray 9-inch springform pan with nonstick cooking spray. Sprinkle corn flake crumbs into bottom of pan.

2 In large bowl, mix ricotta, sugar, flour, vanilla, sour cream, whipped cream and eggs thoroughly with wooden spoon, adding eggs one at a time. Pour batter into pan.

3 Bake 1 hour. Turn off oven; let cheesecake cool in oven 20 minutes. Remove from oven; cool on wire rack. Serve with fruit topping, if desired. Store in refrigerator.

12 servings

MINI CHEESECAKES

WINE-BRAISED PEAR CHANTILLY

WINE-BRAISED PEAR CHANTILLY

MRS. ROBERT WOOD
HOLLY HILL, FLORIDA

4 ripe pears (Anjou, Bartlett or Bosc)

3 cups dry red wine (cabernet, merlot or zinfandel)

2 tablespoons sugar

2 sticks cinnamon

4 whole cloves

1/4 teaspoon ground nutmeg

4 (1/2-inch) slices pound cake

1 cup heavy cream

2 tablespoons powdered sugar

1 teaspoon vanilla

1/4 cup sliced butter-toasted almonds

1 Peel and core pears, leaving stems intact. Place pears in non-reactive Dutch oven with wine, sugar, cinnamon, cloves and nutmeg. Simmer 20 minutes. Remove pears; cool in refrigerator.

2 Simmer wine mixture until reduced to 2 cups syrup. Place cake slices in 4 dessert bowls, splashed with 1/4 cup orange liqueur, if desired.

3 In medium bowl, beat cream at medium speed until soft peaks form. Beat in powdered sugar and vanilla.

4 Place pears upright on cake slices; trim bottoms to stand, if necessary. Remove cinnamon sticks and cloves; pour syrup over pears. Garnish with whipped cream; coat with almond slices. Serve with sweet wine or champagne. Store in refrigerator.

4 servings

CHOCOLATE CARAMEL CHEESECAKE

JENNY DIBLEY
MIDDLEBURY, INDIANA

CRUST

1/2 cup semisweet chocolate chips (3 oz.)

1/3 cup butter

1 1/2 cups old-fashioned or quick-cooking oats

1/2 cup plus 1 tablespoon all-purpose flour

1/4 cup packed brown sugar

FILLING

2 (8-oz.) pkg. cream cheese, softened

2/3 cup sugar

1 teaspoon vanilla

2 eggs

1/2 cup semisweet chocolate chips (3 oz.)

1 cup caramel topping

1 tablespoon all-purpose flour

1/2 cup fudge topping

1/2 cup crushed pecans

1 Heat oven to 350°F. Spray bottom and sides of 9-inch springform pan with nonstick cooking spray.

2 To prepare crust, melt 1/2 cup chocolate chips and butter in large saucepan over low heat; cool slightly. Stir in oats, 1/2 cup flour and brown sugar; mix well. Press firmly into bottom and 1 inch up sides of pan. Bake 10 minutes; cool completely.

3 To prepare filling, beat cream cheese, sugar and vanilla in large bowl at medium speed until creamy. Add eggs one at a time, beating well after each addition. Stir in remaining 1/2 cup chocolate chips. Pour mixture over crust. Combine 1/3 cup of the caramel topping and remaining 1 tablespoon flour; mix well. Spoon mixture over filling; swirl with knife. Bake 40 to 50 minutes or until center is set; cool on wire rack. Refrigerate 6 hours or overnight.

4 To serve, drizzle with remaining 2/3 cup caramel and fudge toppings. Sprinkle pecans over top. Store covered in refrigerator.

12 servings

SOPAIPILLAS

CHERYL BARNA
WOODBRIDGE, VIRGINIA

1 ($\frac{1}{4}$-oz.) pkg. active dry yeast

3 teaspoons sugar

1$\frac{1}{2}$ cups warm water (105°F to 115°F)

1 tablespoon shortening, melted

1 teaspoon baking powder

1 teaspoon salt

4 cups all-purpose flour

Vegetable oil

1 In large bowl, dissolve yeast and 1 teaspoon of the sugar in water; let stand 5 minutes or until bubbly. Add remaining 2 teaspoons sugar, shortening, baking powder, salt and 2 cups of the flour; beat at high speed until smooth. Stir in remaining 2 cups flour to make soft dough.

2 Place dough in greased bowl, turning to grease top. Cover and let rise in warm place 1 hour or until doubled.

3 Fill large pot with 4 inches vegetable oil. Heat to 375°F. Meanwhile, punch dough down. Turn out onto lightly floured surface; let rest 5 minutes. Knead 4 to 5 times. Roll dough to $\frac{1}{4}$ inch thickness; cut into 3-inch squares. Cut each square diagonally to form 2 triangles.

4 Gently drop 2 to 3 dough triangles at a time into oil; turning once. Cook until sopaipillas are golden brown. Drain on paper towels. Serve hot with honey or powdered sugar, if desired. Store in refrigerator.

3 dozen

CLAUDIA'S PUMPKIN-TOFFEE CHEESECAKE

CLAUDIA WENDEL
FRESNO, CALIFORNIA

CRUST

$\frac{1}{4}$ cup melted butter

1$\frac{3}{4}$ cups finely crushed pecan-shortbread

$\frac{1}{3}$ cup toffee bits

CHEESECAKE

3 (8-oz.) pkg. cream cheese, softened

$\frac{3}{4}$ cup packed brown sugar

1 cup sugar

$\frac{3}{4}$ cup solid pack pumpkin puree, blended smooth before measuring

2 large eggs

2 tablespoons cornstarch

$\frac{1}{2}$ teaspoon pumpkin pie spice

$\frac{1}{3}$ cup heavy cream

$\frac{2}{3}$ cup toffee bits

TOPPING

2 cups sour cream

$\frac{1}{4}$ cup sugar

$\frac{1}{2}$ teaspoon vanilla

$\frac{1}{3}$ cup caramel syrup

$\frac{1}{3}$ cup toffee bits

1 Heat oven to 350°F.

2 To prepare crust, in medium bowl, combine butter and cookie crumbs; stir well and press into bottom and slightly up edges of 9-inch springform pan. Sprinkle $\frac{1}{3}$ cup toffee bits over crust. Bake 6 to 8 minutes; do not brown. Set aside to cool or refrigerate until ready to use.

3 To prepare cheesecake, in large bowl, combine cream cheese with brown sugar and 1 cup sugar until creamy. Add pumpkin and eggs; beat until smooth. Beat in cornstarch and pie spice. Stir in cream and $\frac{2}{3}$ cup toffee bits. Pour pumpkin mixture carefully into crust. Bake about 1$\frac{1}{4}$ hours or until nearly set; center will slightly jiggle when shaken.

4 To prepare topping, mix sour cream, $\frac{1}{4}$ cup sugar and vanilla in medium bowl. Remove cake from oven; spread topping on warm cheesecake. Return to oven; bake an additional 8 minutes. Do not brown. Turn oven off; leave cheesecake in oven 1 hour. Refrigerate several hours or overnight. Remove from pan; place on cake platter.

5 Just before serving, drizzle $\frac{1}{3}$ cup caramel syrup over cheesecake; top with $\frac{1}{3}$ cup toffee bits. Garnish with whipped cream, if desired. Store in refrigerator.

16 servings

CLAUDIA'S PUMPKIN-TOFFEE CHEESECAKE

BLACK & WHITE CHEESECAKE

JOYCE QUICK
CANDOR, NEW YORK

PASTRY

6 tablespoons unsalted butter, softened

$^1/_2$ cup sugar

$^3/_4$ teaspoon vanilla

$^1/_8$ teaspoon salt

$^1/_4$ cup plus 2 tablespoons unsweetened cocoa

$^3/_4$ cup all-purpose flour

FILLING

1 cup semisweet chocolate chips (6 oz.)

$^1/_4$ cup water

3 (8-oz.) pkg. cream cheese, softened

$1^1/_4$ cups sugar

$^1/_2$ teaspoon vanilla

2 eggs

1 Heat oven to 350°F.

2 To prepare pastry, in food processor, combine butter, $^1/_2$ cup sugar, $^3/_4$ teaspoon vanilla and salt; process until smooth. Blend in cocoa just until dark smooth paste forms. Mix in flour until just incorporated but still crumbly.

3 Firmly press three-fourths of the pastry into bottom of 9-inch springform pan. Crumble remaining pastry into shallow baking pan.

4 Bake both pans 10 minutes. Remove pan of extra crumbs, bake crust an additional 5 minutes. Cool pans on wire rack. Place cooled crumbs from baking pan in food processor; pulse until pulverized. Store in container; set aside.

5 To prepare filling, melt chocolate chips with water over low heat in small saucepan, stirring occasionally until smooth. Cover saucepan to keep warm; set aside. In large bowl, beat cream cheese at medium speed until smooth. Add $1^1/_4$ cups sugar gradually, beating just until smooth. Add vanilla and eggs, one at a time, beating just until mixed. Set aside 1 cup batter.

6 Pour remaining batter into crust. Stir warm chocolate into reserved batter. Pour thick ring about $^1/_2$ inch from side of pan, on top of plain batter, leaving a "bullseye" of plain batter in center. Pull knife through both batters to marble.

7 Bake 1 hour and 10 minutes or until toothpick inserted in center comes out clean. Run a thin knife carefully around edges to release cake from side of pan. Cool in pan on wire rack; place inverted large bowl over cheesecake on wire rack while cooling. To serve, remove sides of pan. Press reserved pastry crumbs around side of cake, being careful not to get crumbs on top. Store in refrigerator.

12 servings

COOKIES AND CREAM CHEESECAKE WITH WHITE CHOCOLATE

CLAUDIA WENDEL
FRESNO, CALIFORNIA

2 cups finely crushed chocolate or vanilla wafer cookies

3/4 cup plus 3 tablespoons sugar

1/4 cup melted butter

1 (4-oz.) white chocolate baking bar

2 (8-oz.) pkg. cream cheese, softened

1 1/2 cups sour cream

2 eggs

10 cream-filled chocolate sandwich cookies, broken into thirds

1/4 cup all-purpose flour

1 Heat oven to 325°F. Spray 9-inch springform pan with nonstick cooking spray.

2 In medium bowl, mix cookie crumbs and 3 tablespoons of the sugar. Add butter; mix until well blended. Press mixture into pan. Set aside.

3 In small saucepan, melt white chocolate over low heat, stirring frequently, until smooth. Cool slightly. Beat cream cheese until fluffy. Beat in sour cream and remaining 3/4 cup sugar. Add eggs one at a time, beating well after each addition. Stir in melted white chocolate. Toss cookies in flour; fold into cheese mixture carefully.

4 Bake 50 to 60 minutes or until set. Turn oven off. Leave cheesecake in oven 1 hour with oven door partially open. Cool an additional 1 hour on wire rack. Decorate with cream cheese frosting around edges, hiding any cracks with whole or coarsely broken sandwich cookies. Store in refrigerator.

12 servings

APPLE RING DESSERT FRITTERS

GWEN CAMPBELL
STERLING, VIRGINIA

FRITTERS

4 to 6 Granny Smith apples

1 cup all-purpose flour

1 teaspoon baking powder

1 tablespoon sugar

1/4 teaspoon salt

1/4 teaspoon ground cinnamon

1 egg

1/2 cup milk

1 tablespoon vegetable oil

1 tablespoon fresh lemon juice

1 cup flaked coconut

Vegetable oil

TOPPING

1 tablespoon cornstarch

1/4 cup sugar

1/8 teaspoon salt

1 cup water

2 tablespoons vanilla

2 tablespoons butter

1/4 teaspoon nutmeg

1 Peel and core apples; slice into crosswise 1/4-inch rings.

2 In large bowl, mix together flour, baking powder, 1 tablespoon of the sugar, 1/4 teaspoon salt and cinnamon. In a small bowl, lightly beat egg, milk and oil; stir into flour mixture. Stir in lemon juice and coconut.

3 In large pot, heat 3 inches oil to 350°F. Dip each apple ring in batter. Fry in hot oil until golden brown on both sides. Drain on paper towels.

4 To prepare topping, combine cornstarch, 1/4 cup sugar, 1/8 teaspoon salt, water, vanilla, butter and nutmeg in small saucepan. Cook over low heat, stirring frequently, until thickened. Drizzle over fritters. Store in refrigerator.

About 2 dozen

COOL DESSERTS

& SAUCES

GINGER-PEACHY ICE CREAM (page 148)

PEANUT CREAM DREAM

DAWN SLATEM
SALEM, OREGON

8 to 9 whole chocolate-covered graham crackers
or chocolate graham crackers

1 1/2 cups honey-roasted peanuts

1 quart Neapolitan ice cream, softened

1 Line 9-inch springform pan with chocolate-covered graham crackers, breaking crackers as needed to completely cover bottom. Sprinkle honey-roasted peanuts over crackers. Spread Neapolitan ice cream on top. Freeze 2 hours.

2 Top each serving with whipped cream and one spoonful strawberry jam, if desired. Store in refrigerator.

16 servings

LEMON SHERBET ICE CREAM

NANCY WIKE
HUDSONVILLE, MICHIGAN

1 1/4 cups fresh lemon juice

3/4 cup fresh orange juice

4 1/2 cups sugar

2 quarts milk

1 (12-oz.) can evaporated milk

In large bowl, combine lemon juice, orange juice, sugar, milk and evaporated milk; mix until well blended. Freeze according to your ice cream maker's directions. (Do this in two batches.)

About 3 quarts

FROZEN PUDDING SANDWICHES

JUDY MANGES
HORNELL, NEW YORK

1 1/2 cups cold milk

1/2 cup peanut butter

1 (3.4-oz.) pkg. instant vanilla or chocolate pudding mix

24 whole regular or cinnamon graham crackers or 48 chocolate wafer cookies

1 In large bowl, add milk gradually to peanut butter, beating at medium speed until smooth. Add pudding mix; beat slowly on low speed about 2 minutes or until thickened. Let stand 5 minutes.

2 Generously spread filling over one-half of the crackers or cookies. Top with remaining crackers or cookies, pressing lightly and smoothing around edges with spatula. Freeze about 3 hours or until firm. Wrap individual sandwiches in plastic wrap; store in freezer.

12 servings

PEANUT BUTTER ICE CREAM TOPPING

TAMMY RAYNES
NATCHITOCHES, LOUISIANA

1 cup packed brown sugar

1/2 cup light corn syrup

3 tablespoons butter

1/8 teaspoon salt

1 cup creamy peanut butter

1/2 cup evaporated milk

1 Combine brown sugar, syrup, butter and salt in medium microwave-safe dish. Cover and microwave on High 4 minutes or until mixture boils, stirring twice. Add peanut butter; stir until smooth. Stir in milk.

2 Serve warm over ice cream; sprinkle with peanuts, if desired. Cover and store sauce in refrigerator. To reheat, microwave on Medium power 1 to 2 minutes or until thoroughly heated.

About 2 1/2 cups

FROZEN PUDDING SANDWICHES

CHERRY POUND PARFAITS

CHERRY POUND PARFAITS

CHRISTINA THOMPSON
PORTSMOUTH, VIRGINIA

1 (10¾-oz.) frozen pound cake, cut into 1-inch cubes

1 pint cherry or vanilla ice cream

1 (16-oz.) bag frozen dark sweet cherries, thawed

¼ cup chocolate syrup

2 tablespoons chopped walnuts or pecans

Divide one-half of the cake cubes among four parfait glasses. Top with one-half of the ice cream and one-half of the cherries. Repeat layers with remaining cake, ice cream and cherries. Drizzle syrup over each dessert; sprinkle with nuts.

4 servings

PEANUT BUSTER PARFAIT

JUNE POEPPING
QUINCY, ILLINOIS

1 (1-lb. 5-oz.) pkg. brownie mix

½ gallon vanilla ice cream, softened

1 (16-oz.) jar hot fudge sauce

2 cups dry-roasted peanuts

1 Bake brownies in 13x9-inch pan according to package directions. Cool completely on wire rack.

2 Spread vanilla ice cream over cooled brownies. Spoon fudge sauce over ice cream. Sprinkle with peanuts. Freeze 2 hours or until firm. Remove from freezer 15 minutes before serving. Cut into squares.

16 servings

FROZEN MOCHA CHEESECAKE

PAMELA DAVIS
EGG HARBOR, WISCONSIN

1¼ cups chocolate wafer crumbs

¼ cup sugar

¼ cup melted butter

1 (8-oz.) pkg. cream cheese

1 (14-oz.) can sweetened condensed milk

⅔ cup chocolate syrup

1 tablespoon instant coffee, dissolved in ½ teaspoon hot water

2 cups heavy cream, whipped

Chocolate-covered coffee beans

1 Spray 9-inch springform pan with nonstick cooking spray.

2 In large bowl, mix crumbs, sugar and butter. Press mixture firmly into bottom and 1 inch up sides of pan.

3 In another large bowl, beat cream cheese at medium speed until fluffy; add sweetened condensed milk and chocolate syrup. Stir in coffee. Fold in whipped cream. Pour into pan. Freeze at least 6 hours. Garnish with chocolate-covered coffee beans, if desired. Store in freezer.

12 servings

FROZEN CITRUS PIE

CHERYL PETERSON

½ (12-oz.) can frozen concentrated orange juice, lemonade or pink lemonade

1 pint vanilla ice cream, softened

1 (8-oz.) container frozen whipped topping, thawed

1 (6-oz.) graham-cracker pie crust

In large bowl, beat frozen concentrate at high speed about 30 seconds. Blend in ice cream. Fold in whipped topping until smooth. Pour into prepared crust. Freeze until firm.

8 servings

ICE CREAM PIE

JUDY SCHOENING
GREENFIELD, WISCONSIN

3 cups crisp rice cereal

$\frac{1}{3}$ cup maple syrup

$\frac{1}{3}$ cup chunky peanut butter

1 quart ice cream, softened

Ice cream toppings

In large bowl, combine cereal, syrup and peanut butter. Spread in bottom and up sides of 9-inch pie pan. Spread ice cream of choice over crust; add toppings of choice. Cover with aluminum foil; freeze.

12 servings

COOL AND TANGY LIME CREAM SHERBET

GWEN CAMPBELL
STERLING, VIRGINIA

1 ($\frac{1}{4}$ oz.) pkg. sugar-free lime-flavored gelatin

2 cups milk

$\frac{1}{2}$ teaspoon salt

1$\frac{1}{3}$ cups sugar

2 cups half-and-half

6$\frac{1}{4}$ teaspoons grated lime peel

$\frac{1}{2}$ cup fresh lime juice

$\frac{1}{3}$ cup fresh lemon juice

Green food coloring

1 Sprinkle gelatin over $\frac{1}{2}$ cup of the milk in heatproof cup; let stand until softened. Place gelatin mixture over boiling water until gelatin dissolves.

2 In large bowl, combine remaining 1$\frac{1}{2}$ cups milk, salt, sugar, half-and-half, lime peel, lime juice, lemon juice and a few drops of food coloring. Stir together thoroughly. Pour mixture into 15x10x1-inch baking pan; place pan in freezer.

3 When frozen 1 inch from edge, transfer mixture to large chilled bowl; beat at medium speed until smooth. Spread mixture into pan; cover with aluminum foil. Refreeze. Garnish with lime slices.

16 servings

GINGER-PEACHY ICE CREAM

MRS. ROBERT WOOD
HOLLY HILL, FLORIDA

4 ripe peaches*

2 cups half-and-half

2 cups heavy cream

1 teaspoon vanilla

$\frac{1}{2}$ cup sugar

$\frac{1}{4}$ cup chopped crystallized ginger

$\frac{1}{8}$ teaspoon salt

1 Peel, pit and mash peaches. Open pits with nutcrackers or hammer. Discard shells and finely mince kernels, adding them to mashed peaches.

2 In churn, combine half-and-half, cream and vanilla; freeze to slush consistency. Add peach mixture, sugar, ginger and salt. Follow manufacturer's directions to continue freezing ice cream.

TIP *$\frac{1}{4}$ teaspoon almond extract can be substituted for peach kernels.

About 1$\frac{1}{2}$ quarts

PRALINE ICE CREAM SAUCE

TAMMY RAYNES
NATCHITOCHES, LOUISIANA

$\frac{1}{4}$ cup butter

1$\frac{1}{4}$ cups packed brown sugar

$\frac{3}{4}$ cup light corn syrup

3 tablespoons all-purpose flour

1$\frac{1}{2}$ cups chopped pecans

$\frac{2}{3}$ cup evaporated milk

In medium saucepan, melt butter over medium heat. Stir in brown sugar, syrup and flour. Bring mixture to a boil; reduce heat and simmer, stirring constantly with wire whisk, about 5 minutes. Remove from heat; cool 10 minutes. Stir in pecans and evaporated milk. Serve sauce immediately over ice cream.

About 2$\frac{1}{2}$ cups

GINGER-PEACHY ICE CREAM

SWEET TREATS

CINNAMON CHOCOLATE FUDGE, PEPPERMINT STICK
FUDGE, AND PEANUT BUTTER FUDGE (page 160)

BUCKEYES

BUCKEYES

SUSAN KROUNGOLD
YOUNGSVILLE, LOUISIANA

1 cup softened butter

1 lb. creamy peanut butter

1 1/2 (16-oz.) pkg. powdered sugar

1 (1-lb. 4-oz.) pkg. chocolate almond bark

1 Line baking sheet with parchment paper. Beat butter, peanut butter and sugar on medium speed until well blended. Roll into 1-inch balls. Place on baking sheet; refrigerate 30 minutes.

2 In small saucepan, melt chocolate over low heat. Dip each ball halfway into chocolate. Place on parchment paper to set.

About 7 dozen candies

CHOCOLATE TURTLES

VIVIAN NIKANOW
CHICAGO, ILLINOIS

1 (1/2-lb.) bag vanilla caramels

2 tablespoons heavy cream

1 teaspoon vanilla

1 1/2 cups pecan pieces

1 cup semisweet chocolate chips (6 oz.), melted

1 Line 2 baking sheets with aluminum foil; spray with nonstick cooking spray.

2 In medium saucepan, combine caramels and cream. Melt caramels over low heat, stirring frequently. Remove pan from heat; add vanilla. Let mixture cool 10 minutes.

3 Arrange about 30 pecan mounds 1 inch apart on baking sheet. Spoon quarter-size dollops of melted caramel over pecan mounds. Let stand 30 minutes or until caramel mixture is firm. Spoon melted chocolate over caramel; cool about 1 hour or until chocolate is set.

About 30 turtles

VINCE'S GOOF BALLS

MRS. VINCENT ADAMS
HAMMOND, LOUISIANA

1 (14-oz.) can sweetened condensed milk

1 (16-oz.) pkg. powdered sugar

1 (14-oz.) bag flaked coconut

2 cups chopped pecans

10 (1-oz.) squares semisweet chocolate

1 tablespoon shortening

1 In large bowl, combine milk, powdered sugar, coconut and pecans. Work together with hands or spoon until well blended. Cover and refrigerate 3 hours. Roll into 1-inch balls. Arrange on baking sheet; cover and refrigerate at least 8 hours.

2 Line baking sheet with parchment paper. In small saucepan, melt chocolate and shortening over medium-low heat; remove from heat. Using toothpick or 2-tined fork, dip each ball in chocolate; let excess drip into saucepan. Place on baking sheet. Refrigerate in airtight container.

100 goof balls

COW PIES

TAMMY RAYNES
NATCHITOCHES, LOUISIANA

2 cups semisweet chocolate chips (12 oz.)

1 tablespoon shortening

1/2 cup raisins

1/2 cup chopped slivered almonds

In heavy saucepan, melt chocolate chips and shortening over medium-low heat; stir until smooth. Remove from heat; stir in raisins and almonds. Drop by tablespoonfuls onto parchment paper. Refrigerate until ready to serve.

2 dozen

PEPPERMINT STICK FUDGE

KAY SPARKMAN
ALEXANDRIA, VIRGINIA

1 (14-oz.) can sweetened condensed milk

2 tablespoons butter

2½ cups white chocolate chips (14 oz.)

½ teaspoon peppermint extract

1 (16-oz.) bag peppermint candy,
crushed (2¾ cups)

1 Line 8-inch square pan with aluminum foil.

2 In medium saucepan, stir milk and butter over medium-low heat until butter melts. Remove from heat; add chips, stirring until melted and smooth. Stir in peppermint extract and peppermint candy.

3 Spread mixture into pan. Refrigerate 8 hours or until firm enough to cut into small squares. Store airtight with parchment paper between layers.

About 2 dozen

CINNAMON CHOCOLATE FUDGE

MRS. GLENN CAIN
FORT SMITH, ARKANSAS

3 cups sugar

¾ cup butter

⅔ cup evaporated milk

2 cups semisweet chocolate chips (12 oz.)

1 (7-oz.) jar marshmallow creme

1 teaspoon vanilla

1½ teaspoons cinnamon

1 cup nuts (pecans, almonds or black walnuts)

Spray 13x9-inch pan with nonstick cooking spray. In medium saucepan, melt sugar with butter and milk. Bring to a boil 5 to 7 minutes or until mixture reaches soft ball stage. Remove from heat. Add chocolate chips, marshmallow creme, vanilla, cinnamon and nuts. Mix until well blended; pour mixture into pan. Cool completely. Cut into small squares.

About 6 dozen

PEANUT BUTTER FUDGE

TINA YOUNG
ATOKA, OKLAHOMA

2 cups sugar

3 tablespoons butter

1 cup half-and-half

1 cup miniature marshmallows

¼ cup peanut butter

1 teaspoon vanilla

1 Spray 8-inch square pan with nonstick cooking spray. In medium saucepan, combine sugar, butter and half-and-half over medium heat. Cook and stir until mixture reaches soft ball stage. Add marshmallows, peanut butter and vanilla. Stir until marshmallows and peanut butter melt and are thoroughly blended.

2 Pour mixture into pan. Cool. Cut into 2-inch squares.

16 candies

C

1 In
Add
stirr
is th
vani

2 S
or p
1 to
ator

Abo

B

1 H
min

2 P
butt
min
Pou
Spri
Refr
piec

Abo

CINNAMON CHOCOLATE FUDGE,
PEPPERMINT STICK FUDGE,
PEANUT BUTTER FUDGE